AN ONI PRESS PUBLICATION

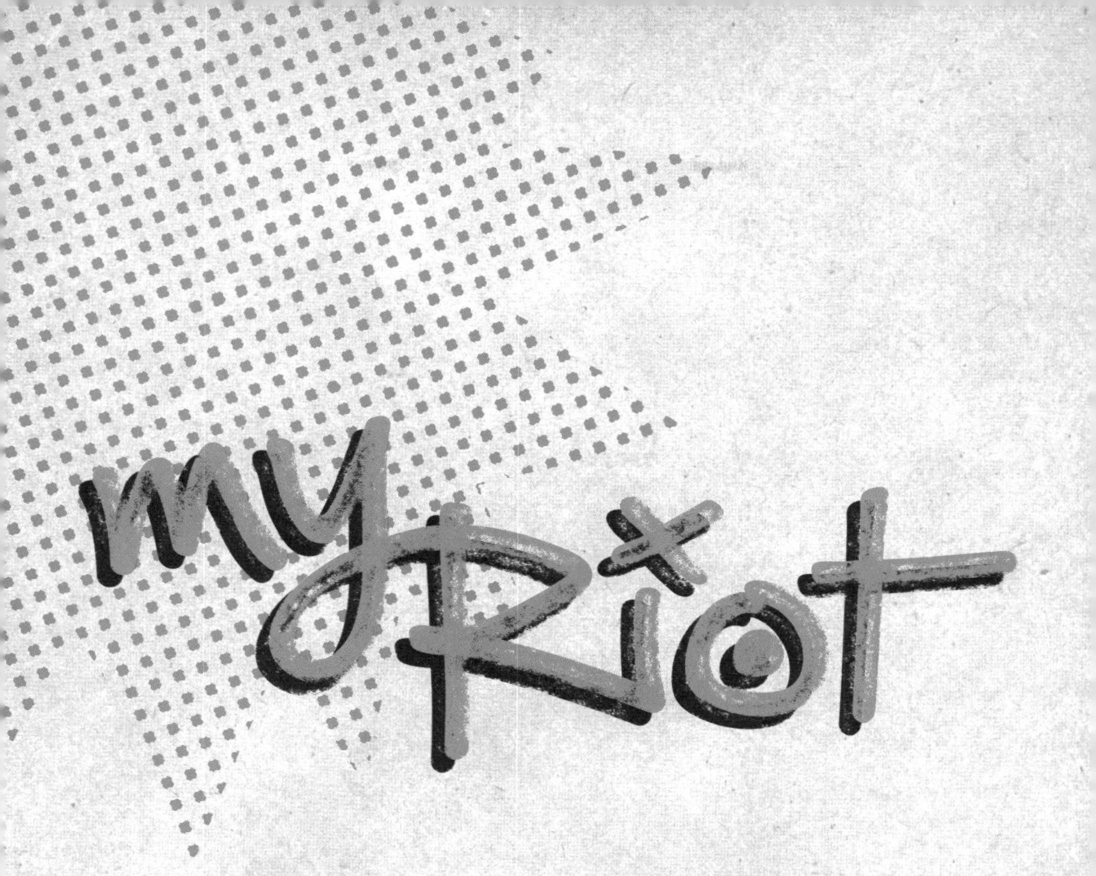

Written by Rick Spears

Art and colors by Emmett Helen

Designed by Sarah Rockwell

Edited by Shawna Gore, Ari Yarwood & Charlie Chu

PUBLISHED BY ONI-LION FORGE PUBLISHING GROUP, LLC James Lucas Jones president & publisher Sarah Gaydos editor in chief Charlie Chu e.v.p. of creative & business development Brad Rooks director of operations Amber O'Neill special projects manager Harris Fish events manager Margot Wood director of marketing & sales Devin Funches sales & marketing manager Katie Sainz marketing manager Tara Lehmann publicist Troy Look director of design & production Kate Z. Stone senior graphic designer Sonja Synak graphic designer Hilary Thompson graphic designer Sarah Rockwell junior graphic designer Angie Knowles digital prepress lead Vincent Kukua digital prepress technician Jasmine Amiri senior editor Shawna Gore senior editor Amanda Meadows senior editor Robert Meyers senior editor, licensing Grace Bornhoft editor Zack Soto editor Chris Cerasi editorial coordinator Steve Ellis vice president of games Ben Eisner game developer Michelle Nguyen executive assistant Jung Lee logistics coordinator Joe Nozemack publisher emeritus

onipress.com | lionforge.com
facebook.com/onipress | facebook.com/lionforge
twitter.com/onipress | twitter.com/lionforge
instagram.com/onipress | instagram.com/lionforge

Rick Spears
instagram/rck_sprs

Emmett Helen
instagram/emmetthelenart

First Edition: September 2020

978-1-62010-776-8
978-1-62010-797-3

Printing numbers:
1 3 5 7 9 10 8 6 4 2

Library of Congress Control Number 2020934139

Printed in South Korea through
Four Colour Print Group,
Louisville, KY.

R0458459150
I'M NOT ADOPTED, BUT SOMETIMES I WISH I WERE.
I RAN AWAY ONCE BUT WENT HOME WHEN I GOT HUNGRY.
I'VE HAD THE CHICKEN POX TWICE.
MY LIFE'S DREAM IS TO BE A BALLERINA, BUT I'M NOT REALLY SURE WHY.
I'VE HAD SEX, BUT I DON'T THINK I'VE EVER BEEN IN LOVE.
I MEAN, I WOULD KNOW SOMETHING LIKE THAT FOR SURE, RIGHT?
HOW AM I DOING?
I'VE NEVER BEEN TO A JOB INTER-VIEW.
WELL, YOU'RE QUITE CANDID.
REALLY?
TOO MUCH INFO?
YOU'LL BE SCOOPING ICE CREAM, MOSTLY.

I REALLY JUST NEED TO KNOW IF YOU'VE EVER BEEN LIKE, CONVICTED OF A *CRIME* OR ANYTHING?
WELL, WHEN I WAS TEN I STOLE A TOOTH FROM A STEGOSAURUS AT THE SMITHSONIAN.
BUT I DIDN'T GET CAUGHT.
MY NAME IS VALERIE SIMMONS. I'M SEVENTEEN YEARS OLD, AND I JUST GOT MY FIRST JOB!
ING
OH CRAP! I'M GONNA BE LATE FOR BALLET.
CHAPTER ONE: A Riot of our Own

I'VE BEEN IN BALLET SINCE I WAS SIX. MY MOM SIGNED ME UP TO LEARN GRACE, POISE, AND DISCIPLINE.
THE CATTINESS, SNOBBERY, AND VENOMOUS BACK-BITING... WELL, THAT WAS JUST AN ADDED BONUS.
THIS IS SARA. SHE'S MY BALLET FRIEND.
LOOK AT THEM.
ALL DUCK WALKING AND KNOCK-KNEED.
THAT MEANS SHE'S MY FRIEND HERE IN CLASS, BUT WE DON'T REALLY HANG OUT IN THE REAL WORLD.
THEY ARE SO CLIQUEY. I HATE THEM.
GOD, WE GET IT ALREADY. YOU'RE THE PRIMA BALLERINA, YOU'VE GOT GREAT TURN OUT... GET OVER YOURSELF.
MAN, THIS THING'S BEEN CUTTING INTO ME ALL DAY AND JUST KILLING.
YOU NEED TO GET A BRA THAT FITS.
THIS ONE DOES... OR IT DID.
YOU'RE NOT ON THE PILL, ARE YOU?
NO.
GOOD. 'CAUSE THE PILL WILL MAKE YOU FAT AS SHIT FOR SURE.

SARA AND I DID HANG OUT ONCE AT HER HOUSE WHEN WE WERE TEN.
SHE SHOWED ME HER DAD'S PORNO STASH. I'D NEVER SEEN PORN BEFORE.
SHE PUT IN A TAPE AND PLAYED IT IN FAST FORWARD.
IT WAS ALL A BLUR OF PINK AND TAN WITH HIGH-PITCH CHIPMUNK GRUNTS.
I REMEMBER THINKING, "SO THIS IS THE BIG SECRET THAT PEOPLE DO, THIS IS SEX?"
AND I WAS STRUCK BY HOW MUCH IT LOOKED LIKE FIGHTING.
WHAT THE HELL ARE YOU DOING?
MOVING MY SEAM SO IT LOOKS LIKE I CAN TURN OUT FURTHER.
YOU'RE GONNA GET CAUGHT.
JUST, SHUT UP.
ALL RIGHT, LADIES, YOU MAY COME IN NOW.

ARABESQUE
PIROUETTE
RELEVÉ
BATTEMENT
DÉVELOPPÉ
ÉCHAPPÉ
SAUTÉ
FOUETTÉ EN TOURNANT
GRAND JETÉ...
MOVES ALL NAMED BY BEAUTIFUL FRENCH WORDS FROM ANOTHER TIME, ANOTHER WORLD.
I LOVE TO DANCE, TO MOVE, TO BREATHE. IT IS MY ESCAPE.
AND SOME DAYS, I THINK IT'S THE ONLY THING KEEPING ME FROM GOING CRAZY.

MISS WILLIAMS...
YES, MA'AM.
PLEASE FIX YOUR SEAM AND DON'T BE CHEAP.
SAVE THE SILLY TRICKS FOR THE PROM, LADIES.
YOU'VE ALL COME HERE TO ME, EACH OF YOU, TO LEARN HOW TO BE DANCERS. AND I'VE NEVER MISLED YOU ON THE DIFFICULTY OF THIS UNDERTAKING.
BALLET IS INCREDIBLY TECHNICAL. IT REQUIRES GRACE, PRECISION, EMOTION, AND STRENGTH.
YOU MUST SURRENDER BODY AND MIND TO IT.
BUT DO THIS. EMBRACE THE COMPETITION. LISTEN, LEARN, AND YOU WILL BE MOLDED INTO MAGNIFICENT DANCERS AND FINE WOMEN.
WOMEN OF SUBSTANCE.

OKAY, THAT WILL BE ALL FOR TODAY.
MISS WINDSOR AND MISS SIMMONS, PLEASE SEE ME IN THE OFFICE BEFORE YOU LEAVE.
WHAT DID YOU DO?
I DON'T KNOW.
MISS WINDSOR, WOULD YOU PLEASE STEP ON THE SCALE AND READ ALOUD THE RESULTS.
UH, ONE HUNDRED AND FOURTEEN POUNDS.
AND NOW YOU, MISS SIMMONS.
ONE HUNDRED AND FIFTEEN POUNDS.
YES, JUST AS I THOUGHT.

WE'RE PLANNING A PRODUCTION OF **SWAN LAKE** FOR OUR SUMMER BALLET.
YOU BOTH ARE EXCEPTIONAL DANCERS, AND I VERY MUCH WANT YOU TO BE A PART OF THIS CONCERT.
HOWEVER, NO MALE DANCER WILL LIFT A GIRL OVER A HUNDRED AND TEN POUNDS, AND FRANKLY, NO PROFESSIONAL COMPANY WOULD EVER EVEN CONSIDER YOU FOR INCLUSION AT YOUR PRESENT STATE OF EXCESS.
IF YOU ARE TRULY DEDICATED TO ME, THIS SCHOOL'S REPUTATION, AND TO YOUR FELLOW DANCERS, YOU BOTH WILL CUT THE EXTRA WEIGHT IMMEDIATELY.
ARE EITHER OF YOU SMOKING?
YES.
NO.
WELL, I WOULD NEVER ENCOURAGE ANYONE TO START SMOKING, BUT IT IS AN EFFECTIVE APPETITE SUPPRESSANT.

WHEN THE FUCK DID I BECOME FAT?
I MEAN, I'VE WEIGHED LIKE A HUNDRED AND EIGHT POUNDS FOR AS LONG AS I CAN REMEMBER.
LOTTO
BE FREE
SURE, MAYBE I'VE PUT ON SOME WEIGHT, BUT REALLY...
MAR
JUST THE GAS?
YEAH.
WAIT, NO, AND A... AND A PACK OF CAMELS.
HOW OLD ARE YOU?
OLD ENOUGH.
GET OUT OF HERE, KID.

CATCH!
YOU STOLE THESE?
ONLY 'CAUSE THEY WOULDN'T SELL 'EM TO ME.
THANKS.
SURE, BUT SMOKING IS LAME.
YOU CAN'T JUST LIGHT UP AND BE COOL.
YOU GOTTA BE COOL, TO BE COOL.
I'M NOT TRYING TO BE COOL...
JUST SKINNY.

ROCK CREEK PARK
THE SHALLOWS.
THIS IS WHERE THE KIDS COME WHEN THEY WANT TO DO THE DIRT.
I USED TO BE SCARED OF THIS PLACE WHEN I WAS YOUNGER.
IT WAS BEING SCARED THAT MADE COMING HERE THE MOST FUN.
NO ONE KNOWS WHO FIRST BUILT THE TREE HOUSE. IT'S BEEN HERE FOREVER, SINCE LIKE THE '70S.
MANY A BUZZ HAS BEEN CAUGHT HERE, MANY VIRTUES UNDONE.
IT'S OUR OWN SECRET LITTLE CORNER OF THE WORLD.
"DO IT IN THE PARK... DO IT AFTER DARK, OH, YEAH... ROCK CREEK PARK, OH, YEAH... ROCK CREEK PARK."

WELCOME TO FLAVOR COUNTRY.
KOFF KOFF
OH MY GOD, IT'S LIKE BREATHING BRIMSTONE!
SO HORRIBLE...
HACK
COME ON... YOU GET USED TO IT, RIGHT?
KOFF
RIGHT...
FUCKING HELL.

HOME, SWEET, ≈COUGH≈ HOME.
VALERIE SIMMONS, YOU REEK OF CIGARETTES!
YOU'RE NOT HANGING OUT WITH KIDS WHO SMOKE, ARE YOU?
NO.
IT'S NOT REALLY A LIE. MY FRIENDS DON'T SMOKE.
WELL, YOU STINK.
SOME OLDER KIDS WERE SMOKING AT THE ARCADE.
WHOLE MILK
OKAY, *THAT* WAS A LIE.
I DON'T LIKE LYING TO MY MOM, BUT SHE NEVER UNDERSTANDS. SHE NEVER EVEN PRETENDS TO.
THE ARCADE?
WHAT ABOUT BALLET?
SOME OF THE GIRLS... WE STOPPED THERE AFTER CLASS.
I LOVE MY MOM, I REALLY DO. I WISH WE WERE STILL CLOSE LIKE WHEN I WAS YOUNGER, BUT SOMETIMES...
WHAT'S TO DO AT AN ARCADE?
VIDEO GAMES, I DON'T KNOW.
...IT'S LIKE WE'RE NOT EVEN FROM THE SAME PLANET.
BOYS, HONEY.
BOYS ARE AT THE ARCADE.

I WISH I COULD TALK TO MY DAD ABOUT BOYS. I MEAN HE IS ONE, RIGHT? HE SHOULD HAVE ALL KINDS OF INSIGHT.
HOW DID THE INTERVIEW GO?
NAILED IT. I START TOMORROW.
BUT HE JUST GOES ON ABOUT HOW, "THEY ONLY WANT ONE THING" AND ACTS LIKE HE'D DIE IF I EVER, I DON'T KNOW, TOUCHED A PENIS.
THAT'S MY LITTLE PRINCESS.
WE SHOULD GO OUT TO CELEBRATE!
JOHN... I SPENT ALL DAY MAKING THIS LASAGNA.
I'M NOT A LITTLE GIRL ANYMORE. I'VE GROWN UP. I WISH HE COULD SEE THAT.
OR WE COULD STAY IN AND HAVE CELEBRATORY LASAGNA!
NICE SAVE, OLD MAN.
LASAGNA. CHRIST, IS SHE TRYING TO FATTEN ME UP?
CAN I BE EXCUSED?
HONEY, YOU HARDLY TOUCHED YOUR FOOD...
YEAH, I'M NOT ALL THAT HUNGRY. I HAD A BIG LUNCH.

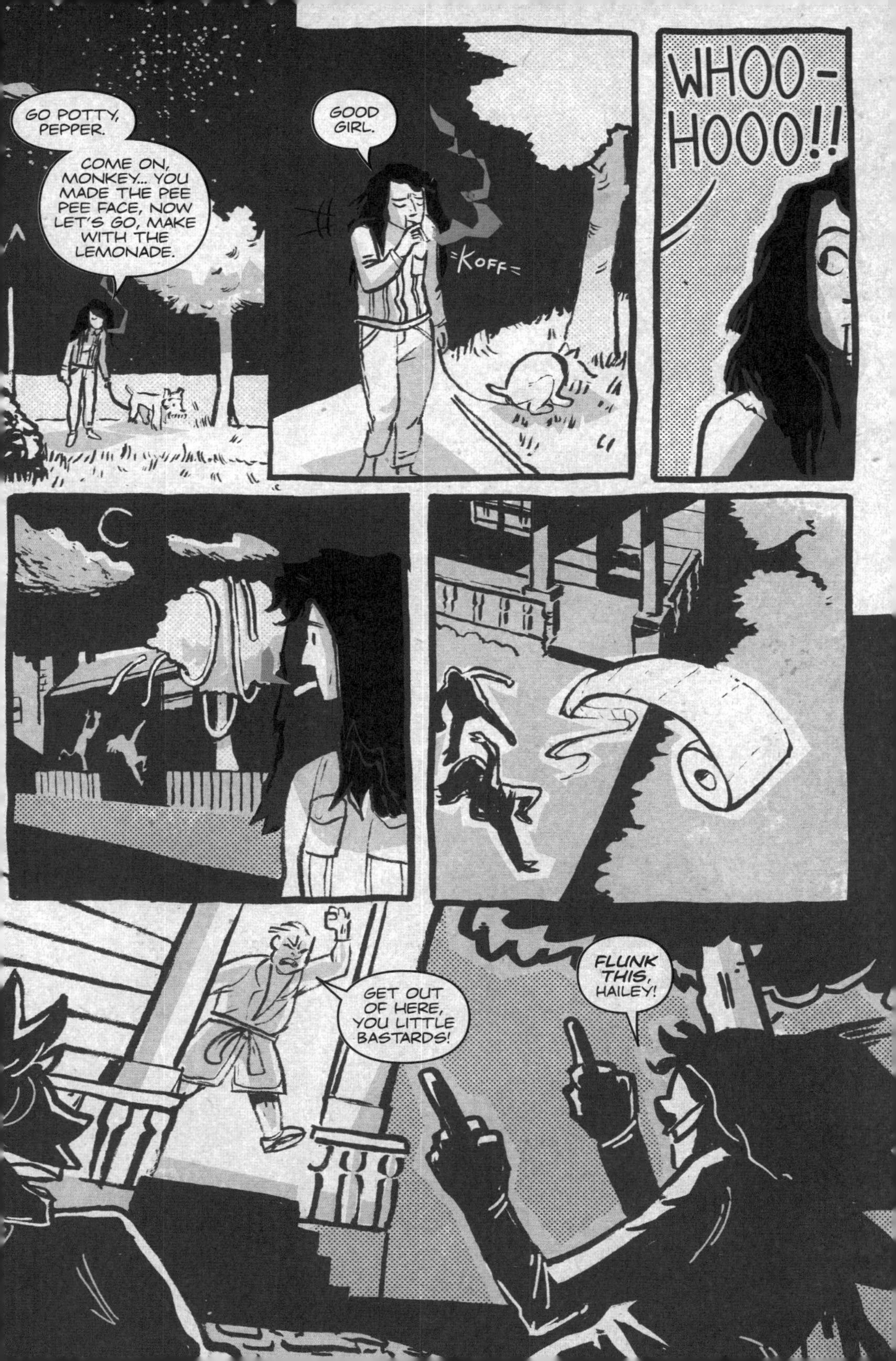
GO POTTY, PEPPER.
COME ON, MONKEY... YOU MADE THE PEE PEE FACE, NOW LET'S GO, MAKE WITH THE LEMONADE.
GOOD GIRL.
=KOFF=
WHOO-HOOO!!
GET OUT OF HERE, YOU LITTLE BASTARDS!
FLUNK THIS, HAILEY!

THE CIGARETTE THIEF.
DON'T TELL!
VALERIE SIMMONS? IS THAT YOU?!
SHIT! PEPPER, RUN!
THERE'S SOMETHING ABOUT BEING CHASED THAT I DON'T GET ENOUGH OF.
WE MADE IT, PEPPER. WE...
CRAP, ARE WE BUSTED? THAT WAS FAST.
VALERIE, GET IN THE HOUSE.

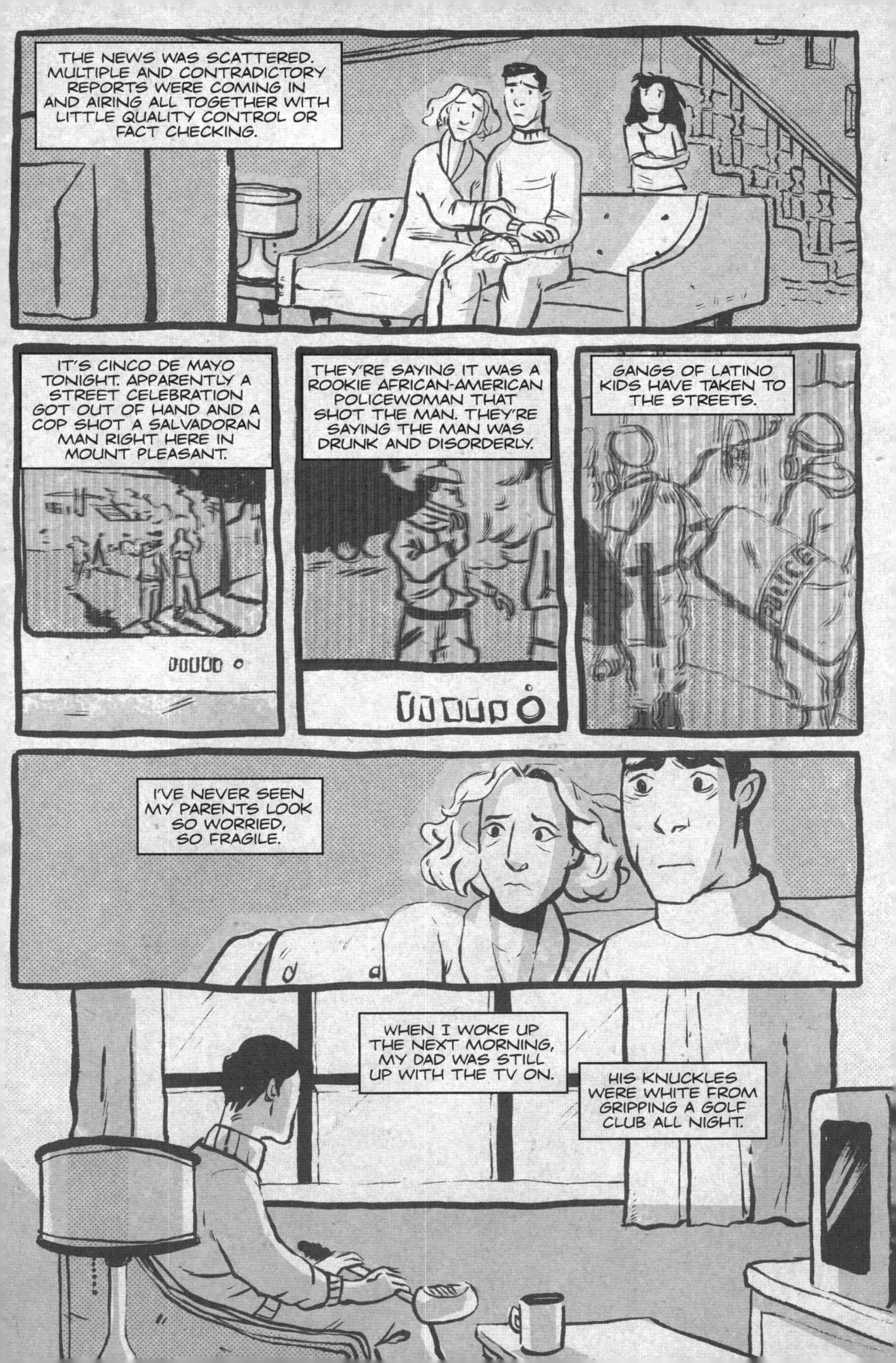
THE NEWS WAS SCATTERED. MULTIPLE AND CONTRADICTORY REPORTS WERE COMING IN AND AIRING ALL TOGETHER WITH LITTLE QUALITY CONTROL OR FACT CHECKING.
IT'S CINCO DE MAYO TONIGHT. APPARENTLY A STREET CELEBRATION GOT OUT OF HAND AND A COP SHOT A SALVADORAN MAN RIGHT HERE IN MOUNT PLEASANT.
THEY'RE SAYING IT WAS A ROOKIE AFRICAN-AMERICAN POLICEWOMAN THAT SHOT THE MAN. THEY'RE SAYING THE MAN WAS DRUNK AND DISORDERLY.
GANGS OF LATINO KIDS HAVE TAKEN TO THE STREETS.
POLICE
I'VE NEVER SEEN MY PARENTS LOOK SO WORRIED, SO FRAGILE.
WHEN I WOKE UP THE NEXT MORNING, MY DAD WAS STILL UP WITH THE TV ON.
HIS KNUCKLES WERE WHITE FROM GRIPPING A GOLF CLUB ALL NIGHT.

AT SCHOOL, ALL ANYONE CAN TALK ABOUT IS THE RIOT.
WELL, ALMOST EVERYONE...
GOOD MORNING, MISS SIMMONS. LET'S GO TALK TO THE PRINCIPAL ABOUT TOILET PAPER, SHALL WE.
TORTURERS OF WITCHES WERE WARNED NOT TO LOOK THEM IN THE EYE, FOR FEAR THE WITCH WOULD THEN BE ABLE TO USE THEIR EVIL MAGIC ON THEM.
BLAH BLAH BLAH BLAH BLAH BLAH BLAH BLAH BLAH BLAH BLAH BLAH
THE TRUTH IS THAT EYE CONTACT MIGHT HAVE LED TO SEEING THE ACCUSED AS A REAL PERSON IN PAIN AND FEELING COMPASSION FOR THEM.
BLAH BLAH BLAH BLAH BLAH BLAH BLAH BLAH BLAH BLAH BLAH BLAH BLAH
I LOOK THEM RIGHT IN THE EYES AND WORK MY CHARM SPELL.
I DON'T KNOW WHO IT WAS, SORRY.
CAN I GO BACK TO CLASS, NOW? THANKS!

LUNCH...
YOU KNOW THE ASPARTAME THEY USE TO "SWEETEN" THAT IS TOTALLY A NEUROTOXIN.
EXCUSE ME?
JUST SAYING...YOU CAN'T REGROW BRAIN CELLS.
BUT WHATEVER.
WHO WAS THAT?
I HAVE NO IDEA.
SLUUH HH-KK!

I DON'T KNOW WHERE THESE TITS CAME FROM.
MY MOM'S A B-CUP, HER MOM WAS A B...
GOD, IT'S LIKE I ATE SOME MAGIC BEANS.
GAHHH --KK!
GAHHH --KK!
BLOUGH!

WHAT'S WRONG WITH ME?
I CAN'T CONCENTRATE.
I MOVE, I GO THROUGH THE MOTIONS, BUT I CAN'T LET GO.
I'M UP IN MY HEAD, SELF-CONSCIOUS.
IT KEEPS ME TERRESTRIAL. IT KEEPS ME MORTAL.
I WANT TO CRY.
BUT INSTEAD I HAVE A CIGARETTE.
WE WERE GONNA GO HIT THE MALL, WANT TO COME WITH?
CAN'T. I GOTTA GO TO WORK.

MY MOM'S ALL FREAKED OUT THAT I HAVE TO WORK TONIGHT. I TRIED TO TALK HER DOWN BUT IT WAS NO USE.
I ONLY GOT OUT WITH THE PROMISE OF CALLING AT THE FIRST SIGN OF TROUBLE, SO DAD CAN RESCUE ME.
I MEAN THE RIOTS WERE LAST NIGHT. THE COPS ARE ON IT NOW, RIGHT?
GARS
CHECKS
I'M SURE EVERYTHING WILL BE FINE.
AND I JUST KEEP TELLING MYSELF THAT.
ICE*KING
IT'S MY HAPPY LITTLE MANTRA.

THE SHOP IS DEAD. ALL THE EXCITEMENT IS ON THE STREET.
LAST NIGHT'S RIOT WAS THE RELEASE OF PENT-UP RACIAL TENSION.
TONIGHT LOOKS LIKE IT'S JUST GONNA BE A FUCKING FREE FOR ALL.
SHIT, NO, NOT MY BIKE.
Saturday Night
THE CIGARETTE THIEF.
HEY YOU'RE THAT GIRL...
YEAH, I THOUGHT THAT WAS YOUR RIDE OUT FRONT. YOU WORK HERE?
I GUESS. I JUST STARTED.
I'M KAT.
VALERIE, VAL...

LISTEN, THANKS FOR NOT RATTING US OUT TO MR. HAILEY.
SURE, WHATEVER.
TIPS
NO, NOT WHATEVER, IT WAS A REAL STAND-UP THING TO DO, AND I'M SORRY FOR JAMMING YOU UP.
DID YOU GET IN MUCH SHIT?
NAH, NOT TOO BAD.
WELL, LOOK... LET ME MAKE IT UP TO YOU. A FRIEND OF MINE, HIS BAND IS PLAYING FRIDAY NIGHT. LET ME TAKE YOU.
OH, I DON'T KNOW.
NO, IT'LL BE FUN.
YOU'LL LOVE IT. YOU'LL SEE.
HOLY SHIT, IT'S POPPING OFF!
I NEVER SAW THE BRICK UNTIL IT WAS PART OF MY LIFE.

EVERYTHING DROPPED INTO SLOW MOTION JUST LIKE THEY SAY...
...AND SUDDENLY TINKERBELL IS SPRINKLING ME WITH FAIRY DUST.
I SMILE KNOWING I'LL BE ABLE TO FLY SOON, AND I'LL NEVER HAVE TO GROW UP.
IT'S LIKE A BAPTISM.
AND CHAOS DANCES IN CELEBRATION.

AS QUICK AS IT HAD STARTED, IT WAS OVER. AND I FREAKED...
OH, MY GOD...
OH, MY GOD...
OH, MY GOD...
WHAT DO I...
WHAT DO WE...
WHAT DO I...
YOU SHOULD SEE YOUR FACE!
FUCKING, "A LA MODE"!
YOU LITTLE BITCH!
NOOOO!
MMMMM, PISTACHIO!

MY NAME IS VALERIE SIMMONS.
I'M PRETTY SURE I JUST LOST MY FIRST JOB.
AND MADE A NEW BEST FRIEND.

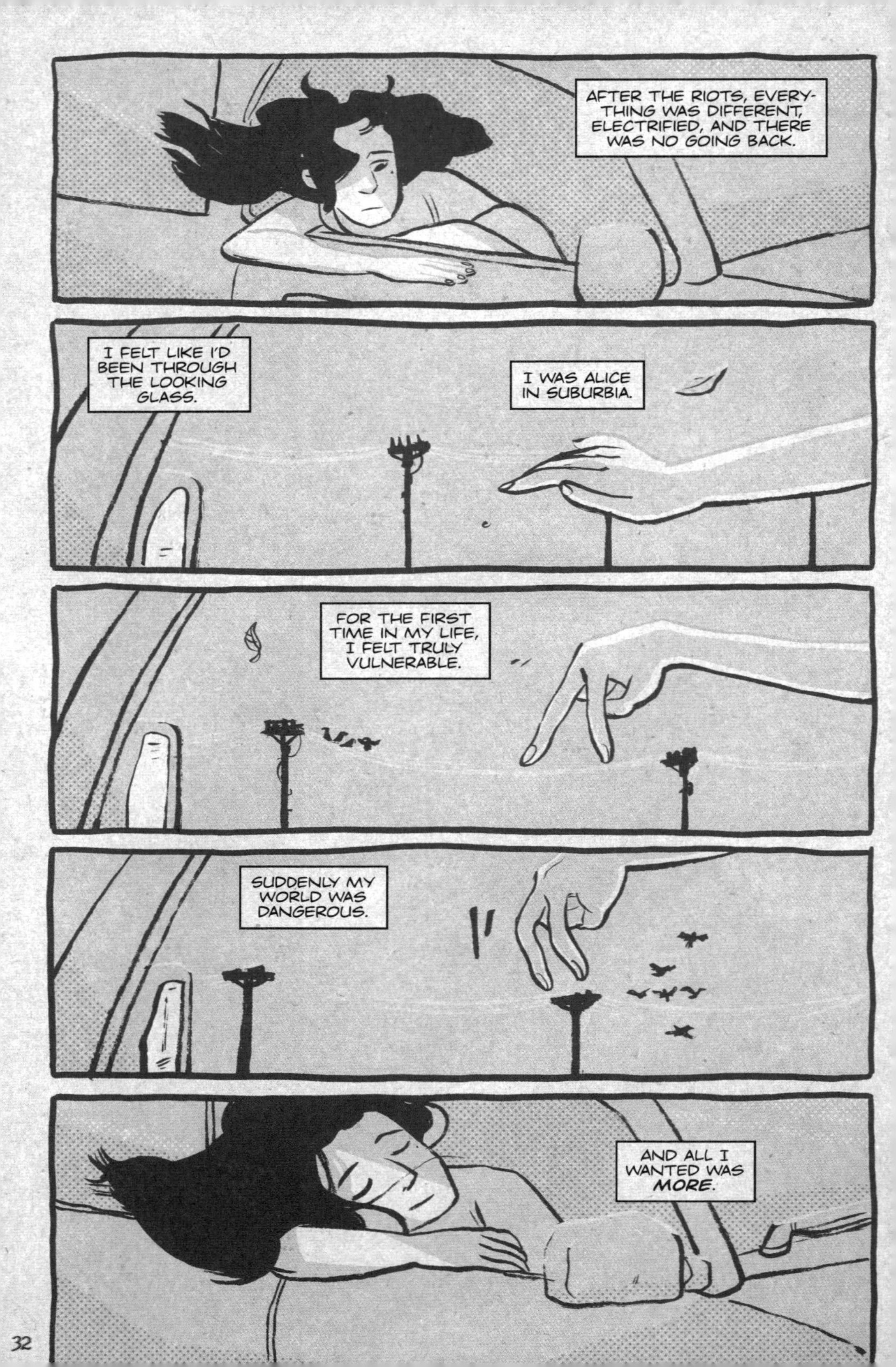
AFTER THE RIOTS, EVERYTHING WAS DIFFERENT, ELECTRIFIED, AND THERE WAS NO GOING BACK.
I FELT LIKE I'D BEEN THROUGH THE LOOKING GLASS.
I WAS ALICE IN SUBURBIA.
FOR THE FIRST TIME IN MY LIFE, I FELT TRULY VULNERABLE.
SUDDENLY MY WORLD WAS DANGEROUS.
AND ALL I WANTED WAS *MORE*.

chapter two:
A Romantic "Pas De Deux"
× ×

SARA'S EYES ARE FIXED AND DILATED LIKE SHE'S ON SOME KINDA DRUG.
WHAT'S GOING ON?
A CLASSIC CASE OF PROXIMAL TESTOSTERONE POISONING.
BOYS!
WHAT?
COME ON!
THEY'RE IN THE BATHROOM. CHANGING!
THEY'RE FROM STERLING.
THEY'RE DANCING SWAN LAKE WITH US.

TODAY, CLASS, YOU WILL BE WORKING ON A ROMANTIC PAS DE DEUX.
WHO CAN TELL ME WHAT A "PAS DE DEUX" IS?
IT'S A DANCE FOR TWO.
KISS ASS...
INDEED, AND SO WE'VE BROUGHT IN SOME FINE YOUNG DANSEURS FOR YOU TO WORK WITH.
YOU THINK THEY STUFF THEIR 'TARDS?
HE HE
IS THAT A GIANT SOCK OR A GIANT...?
...I'M SURE YOU WILL SHOW THEM THE UTMOST HOSPITALITY WHILE THEY ARE WITH US.

GOOD LOOKS, SENSE OF HUMOR, ATTITUDE...
LOTS OF THINGS CAN MAKE A GUY ATTRACTIVE.
BUT THE KILLER, THE LYNCHPIN, IS CONFIDENCE.
GUH--
WHAT IS THE PROBLEM, MISS SIMMONS?
SHE'S NEVER BEEN IN LOVE.
WHAT? SHUT UP!

SHE DANCES LIKE SHE'S NEVER BEEN IN LOVE.
SHUT UP!
SHUT UP!
SHUT UP!
THIS IS A **ROMANTIC** DANCE. IT REQUIRES A **SWOLLEN** HEART.
INDEED.
I MAKE NO PROMISES, BUT I WILL DO MY BEST TO HELP HER.
CONFIDENCE...
GULP
OOOH~
AHHH~
THAT'S ENOUGH OF THAT, LADIES.
BACK TO WORK.
SOMEONE'S GOT A **BOY-FRIEND!**
SHUT UP.

SHALL WE CONTINUE?
WHAT...?
I DON'T LIKE BEING EMBARRASSED.
THAT WAS NOT MY INTENTION.
BUT I CAN SEE THAT YOU'RE HURT, AND SO I APOLOGIZE FOR YOUR BRUISED FEELINGS.
I'M NOT...
IT'S NOT...
IT'S FINE. FORGET IT.
PERHAPS YOU WOULD PERMIT ME A CHANCE TO MAKE IT UP TO YOU?
ARE YOU ASKING ME OUT?
IF I WERE, WOULD YOU SAY YES?
I DON'T KNOW...

MISS SIMMONS, IN MY OFFICE.
HOLD THAT...
I'LL BE RIGHT BACK.
ONE FIFTEEN.
AGAIN...
I'VE BEEN EATING LESS. WORKING OUT...
HAVE YOU DEFECATED TODAY?
UH--
YES, MA'AM.
URINATED RECENTLY?
YES... MA'AM.

I THOUGHT I MADE MYSELF CLEAR, MISS SIMMONS.
YOU DID.
I DID WHAT?
YOU DID... MA'AM.
SIGH...
ANGER, I CAN HANDLE. MAD, I CAN DEAL WITH.
I'M VERY DISAPPOINTED...
DISAPPOINTMENT JUST MAKES ME FEEL LIKE AN ASSHOLE.
GO, GO AND SEND WINDSOR IN.

SOMETHING'S WRONG. CHATTY CATHY'S NEVER THIS QUIET.
MOM, ARE YOU OKAY?
I WAS DOING THE LAUNDRY. PUTTING AWAY YOUR CLOTHES.
WHAT ARE THESE?
SUPER
OH, SHIT...

UH-- CONDOMS.
AND WHY DO YOU HAVE THEM?
THOUGHTS RACING, LIGHT SPEED, BUT NOTHING COMES TO SAVE ME.
ANSWER ME!
SHE LOOKS AT ME, HER DAUGHTER, LIKE I'M A WHORE.
WHAT?!
I'M BEING SAFE!
I'M SO DISGUSTED WITH YOU RIGHT NOW.
MOM...

HEY HONEY, HOW WAS--
OKAY...
DON'T EVEN TALK TO ME.
I'M SO **MAD** I ALMOST **WRECKED** THE CAR.
STUPID CONDOMS. SO WHAT? I DON'T EVEN HAVE A BOYFRIEND!
I CAN'T BELIEVE I'M GETTING BUSTED FOR SEX WHEN I'M NOT EVEN HAVING ANY.
IT'S SO NOT FAIR. I HATE HER.

I GOT CHICKEN... FOR DINNER. SOOO, SHOULD I CALL VAL?
NO. SHE CAN JUST SIT IN HER ROOM FOR A WHILE.
HONEY...
I KNOW. I'M A JERK. JUST HOLD ME.
I FELT MYSELF BECOMING MY MOTHER, HEARING HER VOICE COMING OUT OF MY MOUTH.
AM I A GOOD MOM?
THE BEST. SHE'S LUCKY TO HAVE YOU.
SOMETIMES I DON'T KNOW.
YOU COULD GO TALK TO HER.
IT'S ALWAYS GOOD TO TALK.
OR IS IT SOMETHING YOU WANT ME TO HANDLE?
WHAT HAS SHE DONE THIS TIME?
NO...
NO, I'LL HANDLE IT... GIRL STUFF.

VALERIE, HONEY, CAN I COME IN?
YOU HUNGRY?
DAD GOT CHICKEN. I THOUGHT YOU MIGHT...
EXCUSE ME.
WHERE ARE YOU GOING?
OUT.
BUT I PROMISE NOT TO **FUCK** ANYBODY!
VALERIE SIMMONS, GET BACK HERE!
SLAM

YOU'RE LATE, PUNK.
SHED
JESUS CHRIST, I'M FUCKING SORRY, OKAY?
WHOA, WHOA...
RELAX. IT'S COOL.
I JUST CAN'T TAKE ANOTHER PERSON BEING DISAPPOINTED IN ME TODAY.
YOUR COFFEE JUST GOT COLD IS ALL.
SPAZZ.
FUHHH

SORRY FOR THE FREAK OUT.
WANNA TALK ABOUT IT?
NO.
GOD, THIS IS TERRIBLE.
GOOD, COME ON.
LET'S HAVE SOME FUN. WE'LL FORGET YOUR TROUBLES.
BANG THE DRUMS AND BEAT THEM AWAY!
COME ON!

RUDIE!
WHOA...
HEY! THIS IS MY GIRL, VAL.
BUT YOU'RE BLACK?!
I LIKE THIS ONE. SHE'S QUICK.
!!
NO, SORRY, I MEAN, I THOUGHT SKINHEADS WERE ALL LIKE NAZIS AND SHIT.
I'M A SHARP-- SKINHEADS AGAINST RACIAL PREJUDICE.
WE NEED STAMPS.
CAN YOU HOOK US UP?
SURE, COME HERE.

BAM!
THAT'LL WORK.
C'MON LICK!
OKAY...
THANKS, RUDE.
YEAH, THANKS...
ANYTIME, LADIES.
EEK...
PRETTY LIGHT. JUST TELL 'EM YOU WASHED YOUR HANDS AFTER PEEING OR SOMETHING.

.....
I PEED ON MY HAND.
HA HA
GAHH, GO!
GET LOS
EX
WOW, THIS PLACE IS AWESOME.
ARE YOU KIDDING?
IT'S A SHITHOLE.

FUCKIN SPECIALS
BEER
WHO WERE THEY?
THEY'RE THE "COAT HANGERS."
THEY SIT THERE AND HOLD THEIR BOYFRIENDS' JACKETS WHILE THE BOYS DANCE.
THAT SEEMS KINDA LAME.
BUT SAFE.
SAFE?
HEY, IT'S ASPARTAME.
HI!
IT'S VALERIE, ACTUALLY, AND THIS IS MY FRIEND, KAT.
OH, WE KNOW EACH OTHER.

I GOTTA DO THIS THING, BUT STICK AROUND AFTER.
DON'T WASTE YOUR TIME WITH JAKE. HE'S NOT INTO GIRLS.
HE'S GAY?
STRAIGHT EDGE.
NO SMOKE, NO BOOZE, NO DRUGS, NO SEX, NO FUN.
REALLY?
FANATICALLY.
SEE, ME... I BELIEVE IN MODERATION OF ALL THINGS.
ESPECIALLY *MODERATION*.

HEY, THANKS FOR COMING OUT TONIGHT. WE'RE, UP ABOVE.
HOLY CRAP, HE'S IN THE BAND?!
IT WAS LIKE NOTHING I'D EVER SEEN BEFORE.
LOUD, WILD, AND DANGEROUS, BUT THERE WAS AN ORDER TO IT.
IT FELT OLD, TRIBAL.
IT REMINDED ME OF THE RIOTS.
AND I WANTED TO TRY IT.

I'M GOING IN!
I GOT YOUR BACK!
FOR A MOMENT, WE WEREN'T WHATEVER WE WERE IN THE REAL WORLD.
IN THE PIT, WE WERE JUST *MOTION*.
ALL POTENTIAL TURNED KINETIC.
IT WAS--
OH, SHIT...

YOU OKAY?
YEAH.
GOOD!
STILL SAD?
NO!

THAT'S IT FOR US. NEXT UP IS STRENGTH OF PURPOSE. SO STICK AROUND.
HEY, YOU WERE GREAT OUT THERE. YOU MOVE REAL WELL.
THANKS, I'M A DANCER.
FUCKIN' A.
THERE'S RUDIE. I'LL BE RIGHT BACK.
OH MY GOD! YOU GUYS WERE SO AMAZING!
HEY.
SERIOUSLY, SO MUCH ENERGY, SO RAW.
YOU HAD THE CROWD IN THE PALM OF YOUR HAND.
THANKS!

THE BEAT... IT MADE MY HEART POUND FASTER. SO FAST--
YOU SHOULD FEEL IT FROM THE STAGE.
heh
SO... YOU REALLY DON'T DRINK?
ALCOHOL'S A DEPRESSANT. I DON'T WANT ANYTHING SLOWING ME DOWN.
WHAT ABOUT SEX?
WHAT ABOUT IT?
YOU REALLY DON'T?
I MEAN, IS THAT KIND OF... DIFFICULT?

LOOK, THE STRAIGHT EDGE THING ISN'T A RELIGION. I'M NOT A ZEALOT.
I JUST DON'T THINK FRIVOLOUS SEX IS HEALTHY.
I MEAN, THERE'S PREGNANCY AND IT'S DANGEROUS WITH AIDS AND ALL. BUT...
BUT?
IF I MET THE RIGHT GIRL, AND WE WERE COMMITTED TO EACH OTHER...
THEN I THINK SEX COULD BE A WONDERFUL EXPRESSION OF LOVE.
OH COME ON. THAT'S JUST SOME KINDA **LINE**.
PLAY HARD TO GET SO GIRLS THROW THEMSELVES AT YOU?
NO, IT'S FOR REAL. I DON'T WANT TO TAKE IT FOR GRANTED.
YOU'RE WEIRD.
HE MAKES MY STOMACH NERVOUS AND MY MIND GIDDY.

I WANNA KISS YOU, BUT I DON'T WANT TO BREAK ANY RULES.
OH MY GOD, DID I JUST SAY THAT OUT LOUD?!
HOW ABOUT ON THE CHEEK AND LET'S GET TO KNOW EACH OTHER?
I'M SO USED TO HAM-FISTED BOYS FUMBLING IN THE DARK.
BUT *WAITING* SOMEHOW MAKES IT ALL SO SERIOUS SO FAST.
IT'S SO... *ROMANTIC*.

CHAPTER THREE: CHRYSALIS

FINALLY!
BUSTED.
JUST WHERE THE HELL HAVE YOU BEEN, YOUNG LADY?
WE'VE BEEN WORRIED SICK, HONEY.
I MET A BOY.
HE DOESN'T HAVE SEX. YOU'LL LOVE HIM.
VALERIE, YOU CAN'T JUST LEAVE THIS HOUSE WHENEVER...
YOU'RE GROUNDED!
OKAAAY!
FOR A MONTH... NO TWO MONTHS.
SOUNDS FAIR!

GOOD NIGHT, PARENTAL UNITS!
AND SWEET DREAMS!
IS SHE ON DRUGS?
I THINK SHE'S IN LOVE.
A TEENAGE BOY WHO DOESN'T WANT SEX...
STRANGER THINGS HAVE HAPPENED.

Beep
eep
Beep
6:00
DIE, ENEMY...
I'M RUNNING ON NO SLEEP AND KINDA HUNG OVER, BUT I'VE NEVER DANCED BETTER IN MY LIFE.
THERE'S SOMETHING DIFFERENT ABOUT YOU.
YOU NOTICED.
CARE TO TAKE A GUESS?
I THRIVE ON COMPETITION.
DO YOU NOW?
AND HAVE YOU GIVEN ANY THOUGHT TO MY PROPOSITION?
OH, NO, NO, NO...

YOU ASKED ME WOULD I SAY YES "IF" YOU ASKED ME OUT.
YOU NEVER ACTUALLY ASKED ME OUT.
SO COME ON. ASSUME SOME RISK.
I'M RIGHT HERE. TAKE YOUR BEST SHOT.
ALL RIGHT--
OH...
OH MY...

SO IS THAT A YES THEN?
YEAH... YEAH...
BUT I'M GROUNDED. SO YOU'RE GONNA HAVE TO WAIT.
HOW LONG?
UNTIL I DECIDE TO START ACTING LIKE A PROPER YOUNG LADY.
I'M NOT GOOD AT WAITING.
LET IT MAKE YOUR HEART GROW FONDER.
I MIGHT JUST HATE YOU.
NEVER.

WHO'S THAT BOY?
WE WERE JUST TALKING.
THAT'S NOT WHAT I ASKED.
LOOK, YOU CAN HATE ME OR HELP ME.
I KNOW...
I'VE MADE A DOCTOR'S APPOINTMENT TO PUT YOU ON THE PILL.
BUT YOU STILL HAVE TO USE CONDOMS. WE'LL STOP BY THE DRUGGIST.
I KNOW SHE'S TRYING TO BE COOL.
I KNOW SHE LOVES ME.
STILL, I JUST WANT TO DIE.

PREMIUM
LATEX CONDOMS
24
MOM GRABBED THE BIG BOX. JESUS...
WONDER HOW LONG IT WILL TAKE ME TO USE ALL THESE UP?
...HOW LONG TO USE JUST ONE.
WHEN DO THEY EXPIRE?
I HATE ALL THIS SHIT.
Bee Kind!
IT'S LIKE A DREAM. NO...
LOVE
IT'S LIKE A COMMERCIAL.
IT'S NOT ME.
I HAVE NO IDEA WHO I AM.
I'VE NEVER EVEN THOUGHT ABOUT IT.

I WANT TO CHANGE BUT I'M SCARED.
WHAT WILL PEOPLE THINK OF ME?
WILL THEY LAUGH?
GOD, WHY DO I EVEN CARE? I DON'T KNOW.
I DON'T WANT TO, BUT I DO.
AND IT'S NOT LIKE I WANT TO BE SO DIFFERENT.
I JUST WANT TO BE ME.
BUT COULD ANYONE LOVE THE REAL ME?

BEING GROUNDED IS LIKE BEING ON THE WRONG SIDE OF THE BERLIN WALL.
I CAN ONLY LEAVE THE HOUSE FOR SCHOOL, DANCE, AND TO WALK THE MUTT.
BUT IT ISN'T ALL BAD.
KAT HAS BEEN AIR DROPPING ME THESE TOTALLY AWESOME MIX TAPES.
TURN IT DOWN!
AMAZING SOUNDS... SONGS THAT TALK ABOUT THINGS I ACTUALLY CARE ABOUT AND FEEL.
CONFUSING THINGS ARE SOMEHOW MADE CLEAR IN THE CHAOS OF CLASHING GUITARS.

TRAPPED, I START TO CHANGE MY SPACE.
THESE TAPES BECOME MY SOUNDTRACK.
AND MY ROOM BECOMES LIKE A COCOON.
A SAFE PLACE TO TRY THINGS OUT.
MAKE MISTAKES...
MUTATE, GESTATE, GROW.

I WANT TO START A BAND.
GIRL GOES TO ONE SHOW AND NOW SHE WANTS TO BE IN A BAND.
I'M SERIOUS, YOU AND ME.
BUT WE DON'T KNOW HOW TO PLAY.
I DON'T CARE.
ALL MY LIFE, ALL MY CHOICES HAVE BEEN WHAT MY PARENTS WANTED.
I WANT TO CHOOSE SOMETHING FOR MYSELF.
BUT WE'LL SUCK.
WHO CARES? I'M NOT AFRAID TO SUCK.
I'M AFRAID I'LL NEVER TRY.

BOO!
JESUS.
DID I SCARE YOU?
YEAH.
HEY LISTEN... I NEED A FAVOR.
I NEED A GUITAR.
DO YOU THINK YOU MAYBE HAVE ONE I COULD BORROW?
I'LL BE YOUR BEST FRIEND.
YOU WANT TO PLAY?
I WANT TO LEARN.
THAT'S AWESOME.
WHAT DO YOU WANT, A BASS?
NO, I WANT A GUITAR.

!BARK!!
BARK!
BARK!!
OVER HERE.
BARK!
BARK!!
BARK!!!
I HAVE TO HURRY. I'M ONLY SUPPOSED TO BE WALKING PEPPER.
BARK
BARK
BARK
DOES HE BITE?
YEAH, SHE'S A MISANTHROPE.
IT'S SEEN BETTER DAYS, BUT IT'S WHAT I LEARNED ON.
IS THAT IT?
YOU'RE THE BEST EVER.
BARK!!
BARK!!
THANK YOU!!!
PEPPER, NO BARK! NO!
BARK!
BARK!
BARK!

KWAANNNGGG
EEK...
KWUU-NKKK
GUH...
COME ON...
TWAAOONGG
RAOOOW!
YEAH, I NEED SOME BACKUP, OR MAYBE AN EXORCISM.

HOW DO I NOT SUCK?
IT'S IMPOSSIBLE!
RELAX, IT JUST TAKES PRACTICE.
IT HURTS MY FINGERS.
I HAVE NO IDEA WHAT I'M DOING.
THEY'LL CALLOUS UP.
GIMME YOUR PEN.
LOOK, THESE ARE CHORDS.
JUST PUT YOUR FINGERS ON THE FRET WHERE THE DOTS ARE. IT'S SUPER SIMPLE.
START WITH THESE C, F AND G.
SOMEBODY ONCE SAID ALL YOU NEED TO WRITE A GOOD SONG IS THREE CHORDS AND THE TRUTH.

ARE YOU LISTENING?
YEAH, READY...
TWAAAANNGG
SEE, I DID IT!
I DID ONE! AND IT DIDN'T SOUND TERRIBLE.
GOOD, NOW JUST DO THAT, LIKE, A LOT.
SERIOUSLY, JUST BANG IT OUT EVERY DAY, AND YOU'LL BE PLAYING IN NO TIME.
TWANNGG
I DID IT AGAIN!
HANGING UP NOW...

I PRACTICED EVERY DAY.
JAKE LET ME BORROW SOME OF HIS CHORD BOOKS.
AND KAT PRACTICED ON HER BROTHER'S DRUM KIT.
WE EVEN JAMMED OVER THE PHONE.
WE CALLED OURSELVES ***THE PROPER LADIES***.
SOON WE WERE BANGING OUT COVER SONGS THAT DIDN'T SOUND HALF BAD.

BRIIIING
GO BOBCATS
SO TIRED.
WE CAN NAP FOR LUNCH.
I'M NOT GONNA MAKE IT.
HEY! WHOA...
YOU TWO LOOK LIKE HELL.
#1 TEACHERS
THANKS.
WE WERE UP ALL NIGHT TRYING TO NAIL "I WAS A TEENAGE WEREWOLF."
WELL, THIS MIGHT WAKE YOUR ASSES UP.
THE *TROUBLE BOYS'* VAN BROKE DOWN IN PHILLY, SO WE NEED AN OPENING BAND FOR THIS FRIDAY.

YOU GET OFF BEING GROUNDED BY THEN, RIGHT?
YOU WANT US TO PLAY?
LIKE IN FRONT OF REAL, LIVE HUMANS?
NO!
NO, WAY!
WE'RE NOT READY.
YOU NEVER ARE.
IT'S TOO LATE ANYWAY.
I ALREADY MADE THE FLYERS.
FRIDAY, MAY 17
bad luck benefit show @ BONE-GARDE bar
FEATURING:
UP ABOVE
$5
and introducing:
The Proper Ladies
call TANK for more info 555-6785
PM
ALL AGES
HOLY SHIT.

TOTAL BONE-CHILLING PANIC GRIPS MY SOUL.
KAT AND I ARE ABOUT TO PLAY TO A LIVE AUDIENCE, AND WE'VE NEVER EVEN PLAYED TOGETHER IN THE SAME ROOM.
SUDDENLY, THERE IS NO WASTE IN MY LIFE.
EVERYTHING IS FOCUSED ON ONE GOAL.
"I'M ABOUT TO HAVE A NERVOUS BREAKDOWN!
"MY HEAD REALLY HURTS!"
IF WE CAN SURVIVE FRIDAY NIGHT--
WE CAN DO ANYTHING.

PLOP
I'M SORRY.
FOR WHAT?
FOR LOTS OF THINGS.
YOU'VE CHANGED YOUR HAIR.
DO YOU LIKE IT?
...NOT REALLY.
BUT THEN IT PROBABLY WOULDN'T BE COOL IF I DID.

YOU KNOW YOU CAN ALWAYS COME TO ME WITH ANYTHING.
SHE SAYS IT AND I KNOW SHE WANTS TO MEAN IT.
SHE SO BADLY WANTS THAT TO BE TRUE.
BUT I CAN SEE HER NOSE TWITCH AT THE LINGERING AROMA OF BLEACH AND THE GLINT OF FEAR IN HER EYES.
BUT I'M NOT CRUEL. I GIVE HER WHAT SHE NEEDS.
I KNOW, MOM.
EVERYTHING WILL BE ALL RIGHT.
EVERYTHING WILL BE OKAY.
AND AS SOON AS I CAN, I ESCAPE INTO A WORLD THAT HATES AND FEARS ME.

FREE AT LAST!
COME ON!
LET'S GO!

A NEW LOOK.
A NEW IDENTITY.
IN JUST TWO MONTHS, I'VE BECOME NEARLY UNRECOGNIZABLE.
I BARELY EVEN RECOGNIZE MYSELF.
YOU COOL?
WHOA, YOU LOOK CRAZY PALE.
I THINK I'M GONNA THROW UP.
SHE OKAY?
SHE'S JUST GOT BUTTER-FLIES.

YOU'RE GONNA BE GREAT.
NO, WE'RE NOT.
JUST REMEMBER, THIS IS SUPPOSED TO BE FUN, SO TRY TO ENJOY IT FOR A SECOND OR TWO.
THAT A GIRL.
LET THOSE BUTTERS FLY.
KUH HUHK

OK, LET'S GO BEFORE I THINK ABOUT IT.
DEAD SILENCE AND 100 EYES ALL ON US.
I CHOKE BACK ANOTHER WAVE OF PUKE SO I CAN SPEAK.
ULP
HEY...
WE'RE ***THE PROPER LADIES***, I GUESS.
ONE, TWO!
ONE, TWO!

chapter four:
Queen of THUNDER

IT WAS A MESS OF STUTTERS AND STOPS AS WE STUMBLED THROUGH OUR SET LIST OF ONLY FOUR SONGS.
THE RAMONES, "BLITZKREIG BOP."
THE RUNAWAYS, "CHERRY BOMB."
THE CRAMPS, "I WAS A TEENAGE WEREWOLF."
WHICH WE CHANGED UP TO "TEENAGE SHE-WOLF."
AND FINALLY SIOUXSIE AND THE BANSHEES, "MAKE UP TO BREAK UP"
IT ALL LASTED BARELY A DOZEN MINUTES.
? ? ?

HOW LONG HAVE THEY BEEN PLAYING?
YOU'RE LOOKING AT IT.
REALLY...
THIS WAS OUR FIRST SHOW.
THANKS FOR LISTENING.
HONESTLY, IT WAS ALL A BLUR.
I THINK WE PLAYED SONGS.
I'M PRETTY SURE WE MADE SOUNDS.
THEY DIDN'T THROW FRUIT.
HOW DID WE DO?
IT WAS PRETTY HORRIBLE.
REALLY? WE WERE TERRIBLE?
YOU TOOK THEIR MONEY AND HURT THEIR EARS.
IT WAS FUCKING PUNK ROCK!

AFTER WE HIT RING KING'S.
KING KING'S
JUST IN TIME FOR THE HOT DOUGHNUTS!
THEY COOL IN YOUR STOMACH FOR A TERRIBLE TUMMY ACHE.
IT'S THE BEST PAIN EVER.
THANKS FOR LETTING US OPEN FOR YOU TONIGHT.
SERIOUSLY, YOU WERE DOING US A FAVOR.
KISS ME, YOU DORK.
WE'RE PLAYING AGAIN THURSDAY IF YOU WANT MORE PUNISHMENT.
I GUESS, YEAH, TOTALLY.
COME ON, GO FOR IT.
BUT PROMISE YOU'LL PRACTICE, LIKE CRAZY PRACTICE.
UGH... DEATH BY DOUGHNUT.

MY DAD SAID WE CAN REARRANGE IT ANY WAY WE WANT.
YOU MEAN HE SAID WE COULD CLEAN IT OURSELVES.
HEY, I THINK YOU GUYS MADE THE PAPER.
AND I'M GONNA GET MY DRUMS BACK SOMEDAY, RIGHT?
YOU NEVER PLAY THEM.
THEY'RE STILL MINE.
WHOA... WE GOT A WRITE-UP.
DID THEY SAY WE SUCKED?
THEY SAID IT WAS "RAW" AND CALLED US "SEX KITTENS."
GIRL POWER
GOD, MY PARENTS ARE GOING TO SEE THIS...

JEEZ, NEARLY THE WHOLE ARTICLE IS ABOUT US.
DID YOU EVEN TALK TO HER, THAT REPORTER?
NO. DID YOU?
NO, IT WAS JAKE'S THING.
DAMN, WE TOTALLY STOLE HIS THUNDER.
SO WHAT'S UP WITH YOU AND JAKE, ANYWAY?
...I DON'T KNOW.
AND THERE'S THIS DANCE GUY, DANNY. HE'S SUPER CUTE, BUT JAKE IS... GOD.
HE MAKES MY KNEES GO WEAK.
I JUST DON'T KNOW IF HE'LL EVEN, LIKE, BE MY BOYFRIEND. HE'S SO--
PUT THAT DANNY IN FRONT OF HIM, AND I BET JAKE GETS ON THE TEAM.
HE'S STILL A GUY, RIGHT?
YOU'RE EVIL.
I'M VINCENT MOTHER-FUCKIN' PRICE.

OH MY GOD, YOU CUT YOUR HAIR!
SHUT UP.
STEPFORD SARA HAS NEVER HAD AN INDEPENDENT THOUGHT.
YOU ARE SO DEAD.
SHE'S NEVER GONNA KNOW.
PLEASE, JUST KEEP MOVING. JUST ONCE...
VERY NICE, MISS SIMMONS. I SEE YOU AND MASTER MILLER HAVE FOUND YOUR ***CHEMISTRY***.
YES, MA'AM.
YES, MA'AM.

SO LISTEN, I'M IN THIS BAND.
YOU'RE IN A BAND?
YEAH, AND WE'RE PLAYING THURSDAY. I WANT YOU TO COME.
SURE, BUT THAT'S NOT OUR DATE.
WHY NOT?
BECAUSE I WANT YOUR UNDIVIDED ATTENTION.
CAN WE GO OUT AFTER?
IT'LL BE LATE.
I WON'T TURN INTO A PUMPKIN.
WE'LL SEE.

WE PRACTICE EVERY WAKING MOMENT.
SLOWLY, WE'RE STARTING TO GET BETTER, TIGHTER.
SUDDENLY, DANCE ISN'T MY ONLY ESCAPE.
AND I KEEP CATCHING MY MIND DRIFTING BACK TO PRACTICE, TO THE BAND.
KAT AND I ARE RELENTLESS.
WE'VE ADDED SONGS TO THE SET LIST, AND OUR SOUND IS CLEANING UP.
DANCE HAS BECOME A CHORE, STATIC, OLD, STALE.
I CAN'T HELP BUT WATCH THE CLOCK.
PRACTICE IS WHERE THE FIRE IS.
IT'S HOT AND IT'S MINE.

EXCUSE ME!
EXCUSE ME!
COULD WE...
COULD WE HAVE YOUR AUTOGRAPHS?
WHO? --ME? --US?
YOU'RE THE PROPER LADIES, RIGHT?
PROPER LADIES
WE EVEN MADE OUR OWN T-SHIRTS.
WE HAVE FANS?
WE HAVE FANS!
PROPER LADIES
PIZZA
ROCK STAR.
NO.
YOU CAME.
OF COURSE.
BUT THIS ISN'T REALLY MY SCENE.
AWW, BE BRAVE.

SUDDENLY, IT'S HAPPENING AGAIN, ANOTHER GLORIOUS MESS.
I'M STILL CRAZY NERVOUS BUT DON'T THROW UP.
I EVEN MANAGE TO LOOK AT THE CROWD ONCE OR TWICE.
AHH.. SHIT... GET OFF ME!
HOLD UP! HOLD UP!
HANG ON A SECOND!
HEY, CAN WE, LIKE, MOVE THE MOSH PIT BACK A STEP... SO THE GIRLS CAN BE UP FRONT WITHOUT GETTING MANGLED?
YOU CAN STILL DANCE, JUST GIVE 'EM SOME ROOM.
WHHHOOO!
THANKS!

AS WE FINISHED THE SET...
NO ENTRY
I DON'T KNOW WHAT CAME OVER ME. IT WAS SO SUDDEN AND STRONG.
SSKREEEEEEEE

WHO WAS THAT GUY?
WHAT?
THAT GUY IN THE CROWD.
HE'S A FRIEND.
A FRIEND? WHAT KIND OF FRIEND?
WHAT ABOUT US?
WHAT ABOUT US?
WE CAN DATE, TOO. IF YOU WANT.
I DON'T DATE.
THEN WHAT THE FUCK ARE WE TALKING ABOUT?
IF YOU WANT A COMMITMENT FROM ME...
...YOU NEED TO MAKE A COMMITMENT TO ME.

OKAY.
OKAY.
I'LL SEE YOU AFTER THE SET.
I'LL BE HERE.
UH... VAL...
YOUR... FRIEND... IS... HERE...
SHIT.

WHERE ARE YOU GOING?
LEAVING, ANYWHERE... WHAT DO YOU CARE?
CAN'T WE BE FRIENDS?
FRIENDS DON'T USE YOU TO GET ANOTHER GUY'S ATTENTION.
THAT'S NOT...
DON'T INSULT ME.
AND FOR THE RECORD... I'M A GOOD GUY.
I HOPE HE'S FUCKING WORTH IT.
I'M SORRY.
I DON'T CARE.

I'M SO STUPID.
STUPID AND FAT.
UGHH...
I HAVE TO WEIGH IN TOMORROW AND SEE DANNY. CHRIST.
MAYBE IF I DON'T EAT BREAKFAST OR LUNCH OR EVEN THINK ABOUT FOOD.
DAWN OF THE UNDERFED.
ONLY

BREAKFAST, COFFEE, BLACK.
A+
BEFORE SCHOOL, THREE CIGARETTES.
CHEWING STICK AFTER STICK OF SUGAR-FREE GUM AND TRYING NOT TO THINK ABOUT IT.
LUNCH, DIET COKE AND I TOOK A MIDOL. I DON'T KNOW WHY.
Kate
ON THE WAY HOME, THREE MORE CIGARETTES.

JESUS CHRIST, I'M FUCKING STARVING.
I'LL LOOK IN THE FRIDGE. JUST LOOK.
HIGH FRUCTOSE CORN SYRUP... ARTIFICIAL EVERYTHING...
I GOT YOU SOME OF THOSE BABY CARROTS.
CARROTS ARE JUST BETA-CAROTENE AND SUGAR.
THERE ARE SOME OF THOSE CHIPS YOU LIKE IN THE PANTRY.
I'M MAKING BEEF STROGANOFF FOR DINNER, SO DON'T SPOIL YOUR APPETITE.
MAYBE JUST A COUPLE.
THREE AT THE MOST.
TO TAKE THE EDGE OFF.

CLICK
RIPP!!

FUCK.
CUUUK--
--KK!
CUUUK--
--KK!

HONEY, ARE YOU OKAY?.
I'M FINE.

HE DOESN'T SAY A WORD.
AND I CAN'T EVEN LOOK HIM IN THE EYE.
WE DANCE LIKE SHIT.
WHATEVER CHEMISTRY WE ONCE HAD IS LONG GONE.
WAAHH...
WHAT THE FUCK?
MY MISTAKE.
BULLSHIT, YOU DROPPED ME ON PURPOSE!
IT WAS AN ACCIDENT.
MISS SIMMONS...
JUST ONCE... JUST ONCE... CAN I GET A BREAK?

YOU'RE BRUISED.
OH... YEAH...
I'M IN A BAND.
I... DID A STAGE DIVE.
SIGH...
A TRUE BALLERINA AVOIDS ANY PHYSICAL ACTIVITY THAT MAY AFFECT OR DAMAGE THE AESTHETIC BEAUTY OF THE BODY.
YOU LOOK LIKE YOU GOT BEAT UP.
WELL... I DIDN'T.
VERY WELL.
ON THE SCALE...

ONE THIRTEEN.
I'M DOWN TWO POUNDS.
YOU NEED TO LOSE AT LEAST FIVE MORE.
FIVE MORE?
....
YOU KNOW WHAT?
NO.
EXCUSE ME?
I SAID, NO. NO MORE WEIGHT.
I'M FINE AS I AM.
LOSE THE WEIGHT OR YOU ARE OUT OF SWAN LAKE.

THEN FUCK SWAN LAKE.
AND FUCK YOU.
DON'T YOU DARE WALK AWAY FROM ME WHEN I AM SPEAKING, YOUNG LADY.
VALERIE SIMMONS, YOU GET BACK HERE!
I QUIT!
VAL, WHAT ARE YOU DOING?

ALL RIGHT...
IT'S THE BAND FULL TIME.
YOU QUIT DANCE?
AND I THINK I QUIT SMOKING.
ARE YOU OKAY?
I JUST WANT TO PRACTICE.
GOOD. MY GIRL JESS IS HAVING A PARTY SATURDAY.
SHE ASKED IF WE WOULD PLAY, AND I KINDA ALREADY SAID YES.
OUR FIRST HOUSE PARTY.
BOOM!

KRACKA-
DOOM!!
IT'S TIGHT, HOT, AND WILD.
THIS ISN'T SOME CLUB. NOBODY'S MAKING MONEY.
THERE'S NO STAGE. NO DEMARCATION.
HAPPY BIR
IT'S JUST US AND THEM, TOGETHER.
SHARING A SECRET WRITTEN IN NOISE.
WE'RE THE PROPER LADIES!
AND YOU ARE AWESOME!

YOU WANNA GET OUT OF HERE?
PLIP
PLIP
PLIP
PLIP
KRACKA-DOOM!
HA HA HA!
YOU DIDN'T JUST KISS ME THE OTHER NIGHT BECAUSE OF THAT GUY DID YOU?
HE'S NERVOUS. THAT'S SO CUTE.

IS IT...?
IT'S OKAY.
JUST RELAX.
AND WE DON'T HAVE TO DO ANYTHING YOU DON'T WANT TO.
KRA-KOOM!

Chapter Five:
We're an American Band
PLAYBOY
THE WOMEN OF

SHIT!
I HAVE TO GO!
I CAN'T GET GROUNDED AGAIN!
SO THIS RECORD GUY IS GONNA COME CHECK US OUT WHEN WE PLAY IN RICHMOND.
THAT'S GREAT, BUT I REALLY HAVE TO FLY...
WE'RE PUTTING TOGETHER THIS MINI TOUR, BALTIMORE AND RICHMOND.
YOU SHOULD COME OPEN FOR US.
WHAA...

ARE YOU OKAY?
ARE YOU SERIOUS?
A TOUR!
YEAH. WELL, I MEAN IT'S JUST TWO CITIES.
HOLY SHIT...
WE'VE GOT TO PRACTICE!
SURE, YEAH, OKAY, "SEE YOU LATER, JAKE"...
SHIT, WAIT UP! YOU'RE MY RIDE!

NO WAY!
A TOUR?
YEAH!
OH, AND WE TOTALLY HAD SEX.
GET OUT!
TELL ME EVERY-THING!
NO, WE HAVE TO FOCUS.
THIS IS BAND TIME.
I'LL RESPECT THE PRACTICE TIME, BUT YOU OWE ME SOME DIRT, GIRL.
WHOA, WHAT THE HELL?
AGHHH
I JUST WANT A CIGARETTE SO FUCKING BAD.

SERIOUSLY THOUGH, WE'VE GOT TO GET SUPER SERIOUS.
I WANT TO BE A REAL BAND, NOT JUST A COVER BAND.
I ALWAYS FIGURED WE'D WRITE SOME SONGS SOONER OR LATER.
LAST NIGHT, I COULDN'T SLEEP AND...
WELL...
I WROTE SOMETHING.
A SONG?
SOME, MAYBE... LYRICS.

LAY IT ON ME.
YOU CAN'T LAUGH.
AND THIS IS JUST THE START. IT NEEDS WORK.
I DON'T KNOW...
COME ON, QUIT STALLING.
OKAY...
"I DON'T WANNA PUKE TO BE PRETTY. I WON'T KILL MYSELF TO BE SKINNY.
"MY BODY'S NOT A TEMPLE TO WORSHIP, I JUST WANT TO DANCE!"
"SKINNY BITCH--
"SKINNY BITCH--"
nod nod
...AND WE, LIKE, REPEAT "SKINNY BITCH" A WHOLE BUNCH OF TIMES...
AND THEN IT ENDS WITH...
"HERE I AM. HERE I STAND.
"--EAT YOUR FUCKING HEART OUT!"

THAT WAS...
BE HONEST.
NO, DON'T BE HONEST. JUST BE KIND.
I LOVE IT.
REALLY?
IT'S FUCKING AWESOME.
LET'S WORK OUT SOME MUSIC.
WE CAN START WITH LIKE A, RAT-TAT-TAT-- TOMMY GUN KINDA BEAT.

WRITING MUSIC CHANGED EVERYTHING. WE BECAME A LIVING, BREATHING THING.
A SORT OF SONIC ORGANISM WITH A MISSION.
AND AS WE STARTED TO WRITE SONGS, WE REALIZED WE REALLY HAD A LOT TO SAY.
WHAT DO YOU THINK ABOUT BRINGING IN A BASSIST?
TO FILL OUT THE SOUND, THICKEN IT UP.
BITCH
ANY IDEAS ON WHO WE COULD ASK?
YOU CAN PLUG IN OVER THERE.

WOW, SHE'S REALLY GOOD.
YEAH.
SHE'S KINDA BETTER THAN WE ARE.
DON'T LET ON.
TAP TAP
SO...
SO, OKAY, YEAH... I GUESS YOU CAN BE IN THE BAND.
ON, YOU KNOW, LIKE, A *TRIAL* BASIS.
PROVISIONALLY...
WHAT SHE SAID.
FUCK YOU BOTH.

RUDIE WAS AMAZING.
SHE INTRODUCED US TO A BUNCH OF OLD-SCHOOL SKINHEAD REGGAE.
THE SILVER STARS, THE KURAAS, ERIC DONALDSON... JUST AWESOME STUFF.
WITH RUDIE, WE REALLY GELLED INTO A A UNIT.
HA HA
HA HA
BOING
BOING
AND ARMED WITH ORIGINAL SONGS, WE FELT UNSTOPPABLE.
COME ON!
WE'RE BURNIN' DAYLIGHT.

THERE WAS NO WAY I COULD JUST DISAPPEAR FOR TWO NIGHTS.
FOR FRIDAY, I TOLD MY MOM I WAS SLEEPING OVER AT KAT'S.
SATURDAY NIGHT, I'D CALL IN TO SAY I WAS SLEEPING OVER AT SARA'S.
SARA'S WAS A STRETCH, BUT WHATEVER.
IF I GOT CAUGHT, I GOT CAUGHT. I CAN DO THE TIME FOR THIS IF I HAVE TO.
2 FOR $10.00
maryland is for CRABS
Virginia is for Lovers
BALTIMORE

THERE ARE SOME PRETTY COOL CHICKS LIVING IN BALTIMORE. THEY'RE SO HIP AND PUNK.
I WAS WAY INTIMIDATED AND I GUESS IT SHOWED.
JUST REMEMBER, THEY'RE ALL HERE TO SEE YOU.
RIGHT FROM THE BEGINNING, IT WAS CLEAR THIS WAS DIFFERENT.
WE WEREN'T A COVER BAND ANY MORE. WE WERE A BAND... BAND.
THE ORIGINAL SONGS CHANGED THE ROOM.
CHANGED THE WAY PEOPLE LISTENED.
THESE WEREN'T THE OLD STANDARDS KNOWN BY HEART. EVERY NOTE WAS NEW, BEGGING TO BE HEARD FOR THE FIRST TIME.
IT MADE THE CROWD LEAN INTO IT.

You weren't my first
and you won't be the last!
I'M ON THE PILL,
BABY!
let's have a blast!
WE ALL GOT HERE THE SAME WAY
everyone! everyone!
We all got here the SAME WAY!
Why should I be so
ASHAMED?
we all got here the same way!
by FUCKING!
FUCKING!
UCKING! "FUCKING!" FUCKING! "FUCKING!"
THANKS...
WE'VE GOT ONE MORE, AND THEN UP ABOVE IS NEXT.

SHOW US YOUR TITS!
FUCK YOU!
COME AND GET IT!
SLUT!
IT FELT LIKE BEING PUNCHED IN THE FACE.
I WAS IN A FIGHT AND I DIDN'T EVEN KNOW IT.

CALM DOWN, SHIT!
DON'T FUCKING HOLD ME BACK!
LET IT GO!
YOU'RE OUT OF HERE, ASS-HOLE.
YOU OKAY?
NEVER BETTER.
SORRY ABOUT THAT...
I JUST NEED A SECOND TO FIX MY LIPSTICK.
I FELT...
SLUT
I FELT UNSTOPPABLE.

HI, I REALLY LIKED YOUR BAND.
OH, THANKS.
I DO A ZINE CALLED *XXXCHROMOSOME*. COULD I GIVE YOU SOME COPIES?
SURE, THANKS.
YOU KNOW, I'D LOVE TO DO A REVIEW OF YOUR BAND FOR MY NEXT ISSUE AND MAYBE AN INTERVIEW.
THAT WOULD BE AWESOME.
I SNAPPED SOME GREAT PICTURES OF YOUR SET. I COULD SEND YOU COPIES.
DO YOU GUYS HAVE A DEMO OR ANYTHING?
NO, NOT YET.
BUT I'D LOVE TO SEE THE PICS. I'VE NEVER SEEN MYSELF ON STAGE.
WELL, MY CONTACT INFO IS ALL IN THERE. DROP ME A LINE.
YOU WERE AMAZING. SERIOUSLY!
DEFINITELY!

THESE ARE SO COOL.
XXXC
PATTY HEARST:
RADICAL!!
BRAIN WASHED??
THEY'RE FILLED WITH DRAWINGS, IMAGE COLLAGES, WRITINGS, RAMBLINGS, COMICS, RECORD REVIEWS... ALL XEROXED UP TOTALLY DIY STYLE.
THERE'S A WHOLE THING ON ANITA HILL, AN ESSAY ON THE HYDE AMENDMENT, AND A BIG PIECE ON BIKINI KILL.
ONE ISSUE IS COMPLETELY DEDICATED TO AN ARTICLE ABOUT THIS GIRL BECKY BELL.
BECKY WAS A VICTIM OF SOME LAW IN INDIANA THAT REQUIRED GIRLS UNDER EIGHTEEN TO GET PARENTAL CONSENT BEFORE HAVING AN ABORTION.
BECKY WAS SCARED OF DISAPPOINTING HER PARENTS, SO SHE HAD AN ILLEGAL ABORTION AND DIED FROM A MASSIVE INFECTION.
SHE WAS ONLY SEVENTEEN.
XXXC
BECKY BELL:
THE FIRST KNOWN VICTIM OF
I'M ONLY SEVENTEEN.

JAKE IS BEING ALL MOODY AND QUIET.
HEY... JAKE THE SNAKE, WHAT'S THE HAPPS?
NOTHING.
YOU'RE BEING ALL WEIRDO.
WHAT'S WITH THAT NEW SONG?
WHICH?
THE ONE ABOUT ALL THE FUCKING.
I DON'T KNOW. JUST SOMETHING I'VE BEEN TURNING IN MY HEAD.
I MEAN, IT'S TRUE, RIGHT? EVERYONE IN THE WORLD WAS MADE BY FUCKING.
EVEN, LIKE, MY GRANDPARENTS. IT'S CRAZY AND GROSS.
IS IT SUPPOSED TO BE ABOUT ME?

NO... I MEAN... NO... WHY WOULD YOU THINK THAT?
BECAUSE WE WERE EACH OTHER'S FIRSTS.
RIGHT...
ACTUALLY... YOU...
YOU WEREN'T MY FIRST.
BUT I THOUGHT... I...
I DIDN'T MEAN TO GIVE YOU THAT IMPRESSION IF SOMEHOW I DID.
NO, I JUST... I THOUGHT YOU WERE MORE...
MORE WHAT?

NOTHING, NEVER MIND.
JAKE, THIS DOESN'T HAVE TO BE A THING.
I REALLY LIKE YOU, BUT I HAD A LIFE BEFORE WE MET.
WHATEVER.
JAKE...
I THINK THIS IS THE PLACE.
JAKE?
IT'S FINE.
SURE, EVERYTHING IS TOTALLY FINE.

WE WERE CRASHING AT SOME LOCAL KID'S HOUSE.
HIS PARENTS WERE OUT OF TOWN.
WE DID OUR BEST TO KEEP THINGS COOL AND LOW-KEY, YOU KNOW, BE GOOD GUESTS.
HE GAVE US SLEEPING BAGS AND MADE BREAK-FAST FOR DINNER.
HE WAS SO COOL TO US TOTAL STRANGERS.
JAKE IS BEING A JERK AND NOT TALKING TO ME.
IT'S STUPID FOR HIM TO BE MAD. GUYS ARE SO WEIRD LIKE THAT.
BUT HE'S HURT, AND I DON'T WANT HIM TO BE, SO I PLAY SWEET.
HE'LL COME AROUND.
I HOPE.

"ON THE ROAD AGAIN.
"JUST CAN'T WAIT TO GET ON THE ROAD AGAIN."
A BLACK SKINHEAD SINGING WILLIE NELSON, NOW I'VE SEEN EVERYTHING.
THAT WAS ACTUALLY THE ALVIN AND THE CHIPMUNKS VERSION.
YOU JUST BLEW MY MIND TO BITS!
VAL, LET'S GO!
NEXT STOP, RICHMOND.
RIVER CITY.

JAKE AND UP ABOVE ARE HEADLINING, BUT IT'S CLEAR WHO CAME OUT.
I'M ON THE PILL. BABY!
THE
THE PLACE IS PACKED WITH AMAZING AND BEAUTIFUL PUNK ROCK GIRLS!
THEY'RE WEARING HOMEMADE T-SHIRTS FOR US, AND SOME EVEN BROUGHT BANNERS.
Yeeeee ee!!

KID, I NEED TO HAVE A WORD.
WHAT'S UP?
LOOK. I KNOW YOU GUYS HAVE IT ALL LAID OUT WHO PLAYS WHAT AND WHEN, BUT I WANT THOSE GIRLS TO PLAY LAST.
WHAT ARE YOU TALKING ABOUT?
THEY'RE OUR OPENING ACT.
IT'S LIKE FRICKIN' LADIES NIGHT OUT THERE.
AND YOUR STRAIGHT EDGE GUY'S, THEY AIN'T BUYING ANY BEER.
THAT'S BULLSHIT, MAN.
WE DON'T OPEN FOR THEM--
THEY CAN *BARELY* PLAY!
CANDY
FREE
TUES
SARAH THE SAF WORD
Proper Ladies

I'M NOT GONNA DEBATE IN MY OWN HOUSE, KID.
YOU PLAY FIRST, OR YOU DON'T PLAY.
THEN FUCK IT. WE'RE OUT OF HERE!
PACK IT UP. WE'RE LEAVING.
JAKE, WHAT ARE YOU DOING?
GET THE FUCK OFF ME!
LOOK, SIR. UP ABOVE BROUGHT US IN ON THIS TOUR TO OPEN FOR THEM.
IT WOULDN'T BE RIGHT--
I CAN FUCKING HANDLE THIS, VAL.

WE CAN OPEN AS PLANNED, OR I'M AFRAID WE WON'T BE ABLE TO PLAY AT ALL.
AND WHEN WE GO... ALL THOSE PAYING CUSTOMERS ARE GONNA COME WITH US.
YEAH, WHAT DO I KNOW?
I JUST OWN THE FUCKIN' CLUB.
DO WHATEVER YOU WANT, LITTLE MISS.
BUT DON'T EXPECT TO BE BACK SOON.
NICE SAVE.
KOFF

I CAN FIGHT MY OWN BATTLES.
I WAS JUST TRYING TO HELP.
I DON'T NEED--
--YOUR FUCKING "HELP!"
I DON'T NEED YOU AT ALL.
JAKE, COME ON. RELAX.
NO!
YOU MADE ME COMPROMISE MY SHIT, AND NOW YOU'RE FUCKING UP MY BAND.
I DIDN'T ***MAKE*** YOU DO ***ANY-THING***.
AND I JUST ***SAVED*** THIS FUCKING SHOW.
JUST GET OFF MY ***COATTAILS***.
AND THEN WE'LL SEE HOW FAR YOU GET!

AND BUY YOUR OWN GODDAMN GUITAR!
JAKE...
I HAVE NO WORDS.
THE WORST PART OF IT IS...
I'M NOT THIS GUY.
ALL JEALOUS AND INSECURE...
I'M BETTER THAN THIS. I KNOW IT.
BUT HERE WE ARE.
AND THAT'S WHAT I HATE THE MOST.

GOOD EVENING.
WE'RE THE PROPER LADIES AND WE HAD TO FIGHT TO BE HERE.
I TRIED TO LET JAKE FALL AWAY AND BE IN THE MOMENT.
Everything's not always about you! The world doesn't revolve around ya, SON!
Everything ain't always about YOU! Whoever the FUCK you think you are!
THIS SONG ISN'T ABOUT YOU! OR YOU! OR YOU! OR YOU!

This song is for HER! and ME!
and THEM!
so why can't we just be friends?
THANKS.
I'D LIKE TO INTRODUCE OUR LATEST ADDITION TO THE BAND--
RUDE RUDIE ON BASS.

THIS NEXT ONE IS ABOUT MY DOG.
I HOPE YOU LIKE IT--
THIS SONG IS FOR PEPPER.
SHE IS MY DOG!
THIS IS A DOG SONG.
YOU CAN SING ALONG!
BARK! BARK!
BARK!
BARK!
BARK!
BARK!

You better BELIEVE she BITES!
yeah, that's my PEPPER! she's my BITCH!
IT'S SO GREAT TO SEE ALL THE BEAUTIFUL LADIES IN THE HOUSE.
WE'VE PUT A MAILING LIST UP HERE AT THE FRONT OF THE STAGE...
...IF YOU WANT TO STAY IN TOUCH.
WE'D LIKE TO KNOW WHAT YOU DO, IF YOU HAVE A BAND, WRITE A ZINE, MAKE ART, ANYTHING...
WE WANT TO BE YOUR FANS!

WE SOUNDED GOOD, TIGHT.
WE PLAYED OUR HEARTS OUT.
JAKE'S WORDS REALLY SHOOK ME.
BECAUSE THEY WEREN'T SO FAR FROM THE TRUTH.
WE WERE A NEW BAND AND STILL LEARNING.
HE DID HELP US GET OFF THE GROUND.
BUT I CAN'T LET HIS EGO OR WHATEVER HOLD US BACK.
IT IS TIME TO BUY MY OWN GUITAR.
OKAY, THIS IS OUR LAST SONG...
THANKS FOR COMING OUT! WE COULDN'T BE HERE WITH OUT YOU.

I DON'T WANT TO HOLD YOUR HAND, FOLLOW YOUR LEAD. I'M NOT YOUR LITTLE PRINCESS ANYMORE, DADDY.
NOW I— BLEED!!
I DON'T NEED YOUR PROTECTION, OR YOUR WEAK ERECTION. I'VE GOT MY BEARINGS. A NEW DIRECTION.
..I'M on the ROAD! IN the ZONE! On MY WAY! ON MY OWN!!
STICK AROUND. UP ABOVE IS NEXT, AND WE LOVE THEM.

I'VE SEEN THEM PLAY PLENTY BY NOW, BUT I'VE NEVER SEEN THEM SO ON POINT.
JAKE WAS POSSESSED.
IT REMINDS ME OF THE FIRST TIME I SAW HIM PLAY. AND I SUDDENLY REALIZE THIS MIGHT BE THE LAST.
SOME GUY WANTS TO TALK TO US.
I THINK HE'S THAT RECORD EXEC...
WHERE'S RUDIE?
SHE DUCKED OUT TO SMOKE UP WITH SOME CHICKS.

THIS IS THE MAJOR LABEL GUY THAT HAS COME TO SEE JAKE.
HE OFFERS US A CONTRACT ON THE SPOT.
SAYS THEY ARE LOOKING TO GET INTO THIS NEW "RIOT GIRL" THING.
THE CATCH IS... AND THERE'S ALWAYS A CATCH, RIGHT?
HE SAYS WE HAVE TO CUT RUDIE AND FIND A "CUTE" BASS PLAYER.
BUT HE WANTS TO, YOU KNOW, MAINTAIN THE "GIRL POWER SHTICK."
I MEAN, YOU'D IMAGINE IT WOULD BE LIKE SOME GRAND FAUSTIAN THING WITH LIKE MILLIONS OF DOLLARS ON THE LINE FOR YOUR SOUL.
I THINK WHAT BURNS ME THE MOST IS HOW UNINSPIRED HIS OFFER TO SELL OUT IS.
BUT IT ISN'T LIKE THAT AT ALL.

IT'S SO SIMPLE, JUST MARKETING.
A DEAF, TOOTHLESS SHARK TRYING TO MAKE A BUCK WITHOUT REALLY MAKING ANYTHING.
WHAT CINCHES IT THOUGH... HE REEKS OF CIGARS AND I DON'T KNOW, LIKE DRY CLEANING CHEMICALS.
THE SMELLS MIX INTO SOMETHING AKIN TO FORMALDEHYDE.
HE SMELLS LIKE DEATH.
KOFF KOFF
OH SHIT.
RUDIE!

I'VE BEEN HERE BEFORE.
SLOW MOTION LAND.
A RIOT.

chapter six:
Legends Never Die

I'D NEVER BEEN IN A REAL FIGHT BEFORE.
IT WAS TERRIFYING BUT EXHILARATING.
P-TOO
AND HURT LIKE HELL.
DUDE. WE KICKED ASS TONIGHT!
HA! HA! HA!
HA! HA! OUCH! OH, GOD...
A BIT THEATRICAL BUT IT FELT NECESSARY.
ONE FOR ALL.
AND ALL FOR ONE!

BEING BACK HOME WAS LIKE STEPPING OFF A ROLLER COASTER.
YOUR FEET ARE ON SOLID GROUND, BUT YOU FEEL LIKE YOU'RE STILL MOVING.

TELL ME NOW, IS YOUR FATHER PLANNING A SURPRISE PARTY FOR ME?
I HAVE NO IDEA WHAT YOU ARE TALKING ABOUT.
YOU BOTH ARE TERRIBLE LIARS.
hee
SURPRISE!
OH, MY GOODNESS! YOU GUYS...

DID YOU EXPECT ANYTHING?
NO, NOT A CLUE.
HOW DID YOU PULL ALL THIS OFF?
I HAD A GREAT HELPER.
OK, WOW...
PLAYING IN FRONT OF PEOPLE YOU KNOW IS TOTALLY WORSE THAN PLAYING FOR STRANGERS.
SO, I WROTE THIS FOR YOU, MOM.
HAPPY BIRTHDAY.
SHE'S REALLY GOOD.
SHE'S AMAZING.

OKAY, THAT'S IT. UH... IT'S KINDA UNFINISHED.
THE LYRICS NEED WORK, BUT WELL, I HOPE YOU LIKE IT.
THAT WAS MOST WONDERFUL PRESENT EVER.
THANK YOU.
SO WHAT'S NEXT FOR THE BAND?
WE'VE BEEN INVITED TO PLAY AT THIS REALLY BIG MUSIC FESTIVAL.
THAT'S AMAZING, HONEY. WHERE?
OLYMPIA, WASHINGTON.
WASHINGTON... THE STATE?
THAT'S THE OTHER SIDE OF THE COUNTRY--
I KNOW, BUT WE'VE GOT A PLAN.

WE'RE SETTING UP SHOWS FOR A TOUR TO MAKE ENOUGH MONEY TO GET US THERE AND BACK AND COVER GAS, FOOD, AND RENTING A VAN.
AND IT'LL BE SUMMER. I WON'T MISS ANY SCHOOL...
SWEETHEART, THAT'S A LONG WAY TO TRAVEL AND, REALLY, ANYTHING COULD GO WRONG.
NO...
I THINK WE SHOULD LET HER GO.
SHE'S GROWN UP, JOHN.
SHE CAN HANDLE IT.
WAIT, SO YOU'RE LETTING ME GO?
WE STILL NEED TO FIGURE OUT ALL THE DETAILS BUT...
YES.
OH, MY GOD! YOU ARE THE BEST MOM EVER!
BUT YOU HAVE TO CALL HOME TWICE A DAY.

BEEP
BEEP
I HAVE TO CALL KAT!
THREE TIMES!
THREE CALLS A DAY!
YOU ARE JUST FULL OF SURPRISES TODAY.
SHE'S A GOOD GIRL, AND SHE'S TALENTED, AND SHE'S SMART.
SO SMART.
BUT DON'T MISTAKE ME.
IT'S REALLY HARD TO LET HER GO.
SHE WAS SAFE INSIDE ME JUST SECONDS AGO.
HAPPY BIRTHDAY.

NEED A HAND?
Z
NO, I GOT IT!
BA'M
GO WEST, YOUNG MAN!
GO WEST!

WE'D REACHED OUT TO GIRLS WE'D MET THROUGH BANDS WE KNEW AND ZINES WE LIKED.
THEY HELPED US OUT AS WE WENT.
THEY FED US.
LASAGNA! MY FAVORITE.
GAVE US SHELTER.
DO YOU NEED A TOOTH BRUSH?
I'M GOOD, THANKS.
GAS MONEY, BEER...
YOU REALLY DON'T...
WE GOT IT.
WE WANT TO.
THEY PASSED US ALONG FROM ONE TOWN TO THE NEXT, THESE AMAZING WOMEN.
PROPER LADIES
Welcome Ladies!
WE CROSSED THE COUNTRY BY CRASHING ON COUCHES.
BLURRING THE LINES BETWEEN FANS AND FRIENDS.

WE PLAYED IN PEOPLE'S HOMES, IN BACKYARDS, AT PARTIES.
ONE TIME WE EVEN PLAYED RIGHT OUT IN THE STREET.
WE PLAYED FOR THEM.
AND THEY PLAYED FOR US.
SOME GIRLS FORMING BANDS JUST DAYS BEFORE.
THANKS! WE'RE THE STERILE CUCKOOS!
THIS IS OUR FIRST SHOW, BUT DEFINITELY NOT OUR LAST!

WE COLLECTED T-SHIRTS FROM OTHER BANDS AND CONSTANTLY TRADED CLOTHES.
WE BECAME *NEW* PEOPLE. A COLLECTION OF EVERYONE WE MET.
WE LIVED LIKE NOMADS.
WE WERE VAGABONDS, BOHEMIANS.
"AS A WOMAN, I HAVE NO COUNTRY. AS A WOMAN, MY COUNTRY IS THE WHOLE WORLD."
VIRGINIA WOOLF selected essays
WE WERE SEEING THE WORLD FOR THE FIRST TIME.
AND IT WAS SO MUCH MORE WEIRD AND WONDERFUL THAN I COULD HAVE IMAGINED.

WE BOUGHT A REFURBISHED 4-TRACK IN ILLINOIS AND A CASE OF CASSETTES.
OUR FIRST TAPE!
DOES THIS COUNT AS BEING **PUBLISHED** MUSICIANS?
FUCK YEAH IT DOES!
WHAT MAKES IT MORE **REAL** JUST CAUSE SOMEONE ELSE DOES IT?
IF YOU WANT IT DONE RIGHT...
DO IT YOURSELF.
Proper Ladies
WE LEARNED HOW TO SCREEN PRINT IN WISCONSIN.
TAKE YOUR SQUEEGEE AND MAKE ONE SMOOTH MOVEMENT DOWN THE SCREEN, EXERTING STRONG PRESSURE.
LIKE THIS?
WE LIVED OFF OUR ART.
HANDMADE TEES AND TAPES!
THANKS! ENJOY!
Fuck Manners
Fuck Manners
T-SHIRTS $10

EVERY JOURNEY HAS A DESTINATION, AND OURS WAS NO DIFFERENT.
OLYMPIA.

IT WAS A COMMUNITY-BASED, NOT-FOR-PROFIT MUSIC AND ARTS FESTIVAL FOR FEMINIST AND WOMEN ARTISTS CONCEIVED AND EXECUTED BY WOMEN.
ALL OUR HEROES WERE THERE, BIKINI KILL, BRATMOBILE, SLEATER-KINNEY--
IT WAS A GATHERING OF TITANS.
ALL THESE BANDS, ALL THESE WOMEN COMING TOGETHER TO ENTERTAIN AND EMPOWER ONE ANOTHER.
IT TOOK MY BREATH AWAY.

FINALLY IT WAS OUR TURN TO PLAY.
HOLY SHIT...
THE ROAD HAD MATURED US.
ALL THE PRETENSION AND POSE WAS GONE. WE WERE CONDUITS NOW.

WE SIMPLY OPENED UP AND LET THE MUSIC COME THROUGH US.
I DIDN'T KNOW IT AT THE TIME, BUT THAT WAS OUR MOMENT IN THE SUN.

IT WAS AMAZING, MOM!
ALMOST TOO PERFECT TO BE TRUE.
PHONE
IT WAS LIKE A DREAM!
THE BEST DREAM EVER!
I WISH YOU COULD HAVE BEEN THERE TO SEE IT!
KWIKIE
IT'S SO BIG, MOM. THE WORLD!
SO BIG I CAN HARDLY STAND IT!
KWIKIE!
I LOVE YOU SO MUCH, AND POP TOO!
I GOTTA RUN!

WAS THAT VAL?
YES.
WELL HOW DID THE BIG SHOW GO? IS SHE HAVING FUN?
WHEN'S SHE COMING HOME?
OH, YOU SWEET, DARLING MAN.
SHE'S NOT COMING HOME.

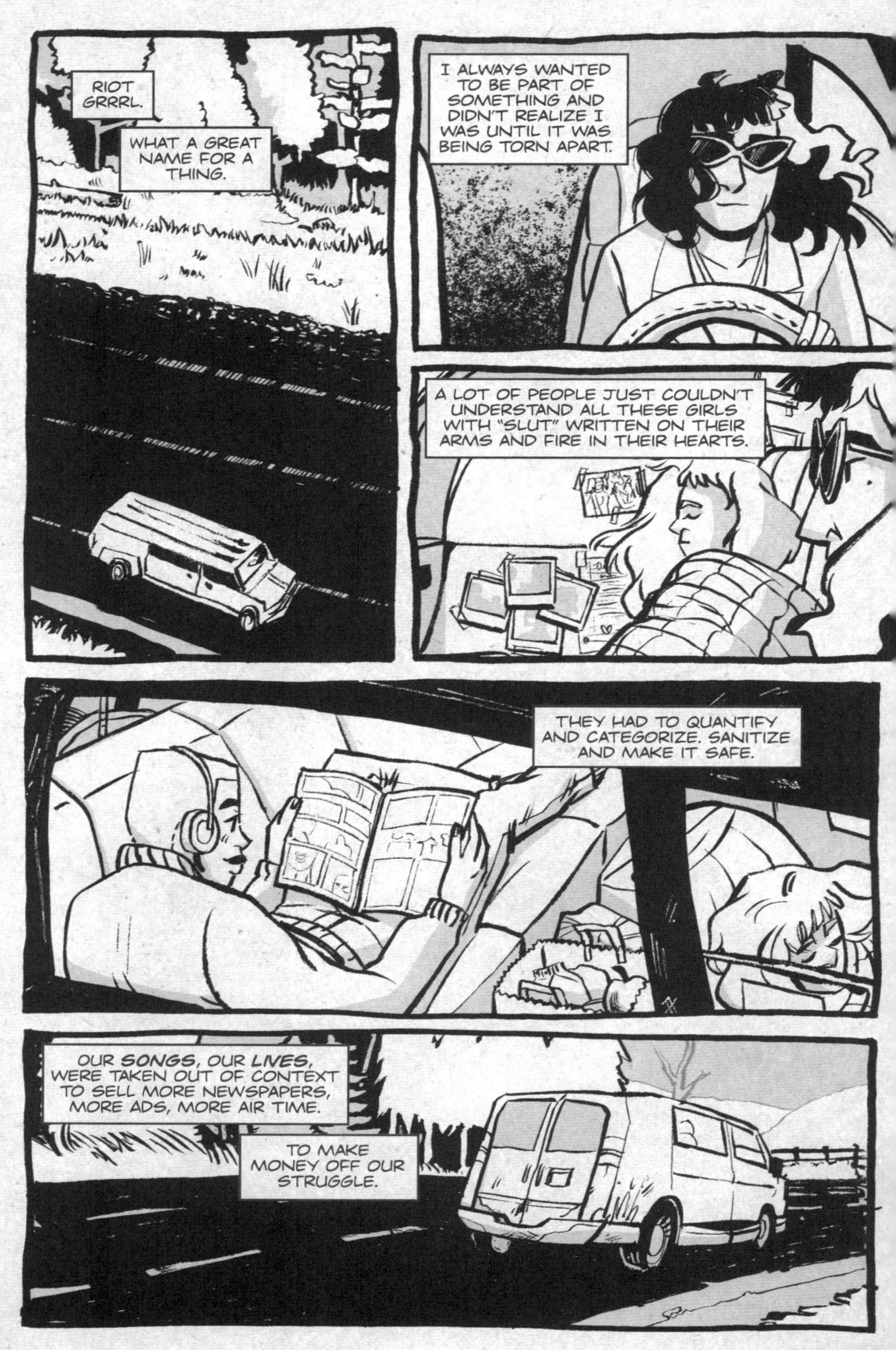
RIOT GRRRL.
WHAT A GREAT NAME FOR A THING.
I ALWAYS WANTED TO BE PART OF SOMETHING AND DIDN'T REALIZE I WAS UNTIL IT WAS BEING TORN APART.
A LOT OF PEOPLE JUST COULDN'T UNDERSTAND ALL THESE GIRLS WITH "SLUT" WRITTEN ON THEIR ARMS AND FIRE IN THEIR HEARTS.
THEY HAD TO QUANTIFY AND CATEGORIZE. SANITIZE AND MAKE IT SAFE.
OUR *SONGS*, OUR *LIVES*, WERE TAKEN OUT OF CONTEXT TO SELL MORE NEWSPAPERS, MORE ADS, MORE AIR TIME.
TO MAKE MONEY OFF OUR STRUGGLE.

THE TRUTH GOT ALL TWISTED UP AND WARPED UNTIL IT WAS UNRECOGNIZABLE.
BUT THERE WAS PLENTY OF BLAME TO GO AROUND.
PETTINESS, JEALOUSY, INFIGHTING...
IT'S WEIRD THAT SOMEONE YOU'VE NEVER MET COULD HATE YOU.
WE GOT ANOTHER DEAL FROM AN INDIE LABEL AND PUT OUT TWO PRETTY DECENT ALBUMS.
WE EVEN GOT TO TOUR EUROPE.
BUSKING IN PARIS, CLUBBING IN ITALY, NEARLY ARRESTED IN GERMANY...
IT WAS HARD, AND WONDERFUL, AND TERRIBLE, AND AMAZING.

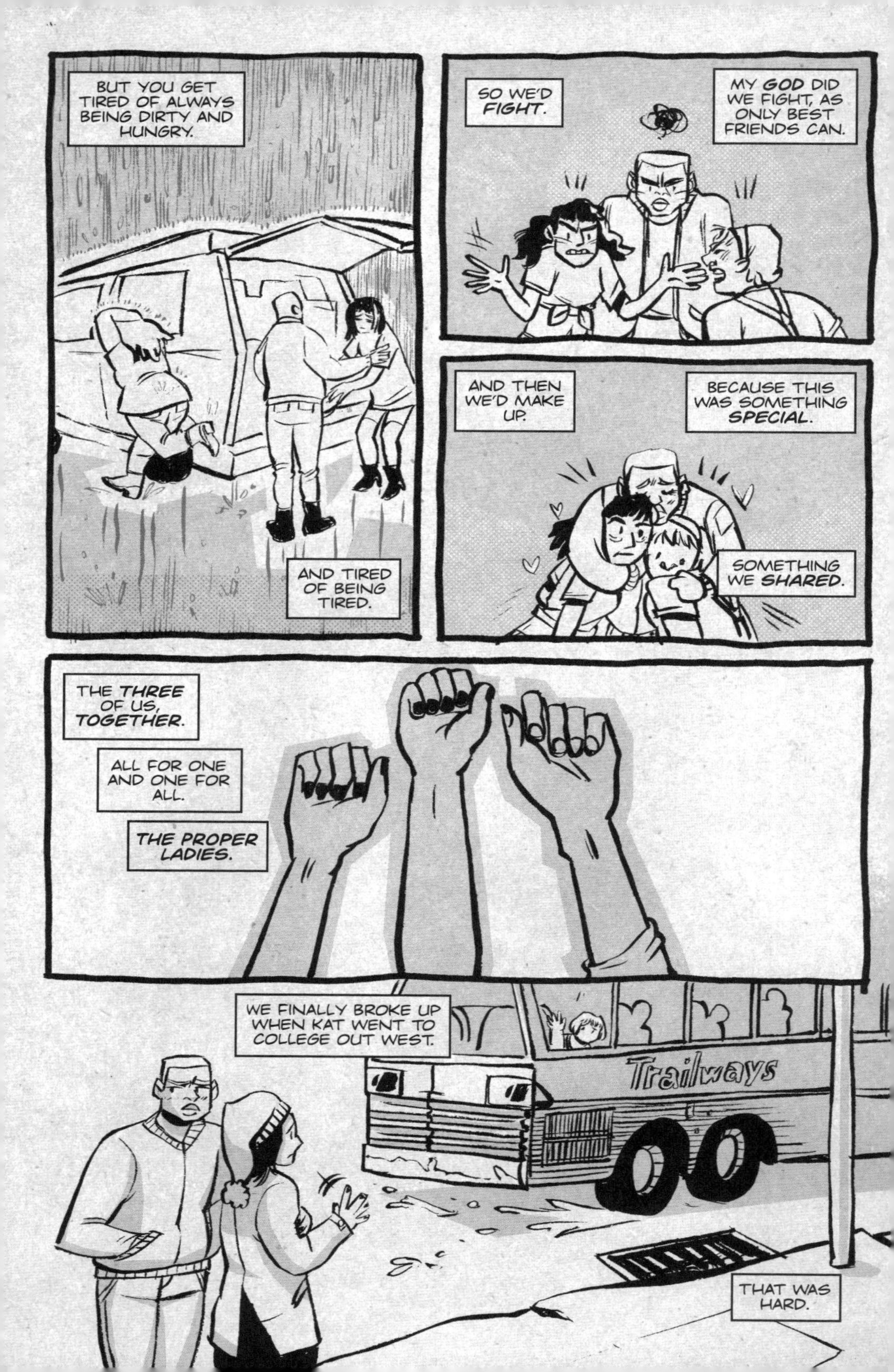
BUT YOU GET TIRED OF ALWAYS BEING DIRTY AND HUNGRY.
AND TIRED OF BEING TIRED.
SO WE'D FIGHT.
MY GOD DID WE FIGHT, AS ONLY BEST FRIENDS CAN.
AND THEN WE'D MAKE UP.
BECAUSE THIS WAS SOMETHING SPECIAL.
SOMETHING WE SHARED.
THE THREE OF US, TOGETHER.
ALL FOR ONE AND ONE FOR ALL.
THE PROPER LADIES.
WE FINALLY BROKE UP WHEN KAT WENT TO COLLEGE OUT WEST.
Trailways
THAT WAS HARD.

I MOVED TO BROOKLYN AND STARTED ANOTHER BAND, THEORY AND ACTION.
JAKE'S IN N.Y. TOO. WE RUN INTO EACH OTHER NOW AND THEN.
WE'RE OLDER NOW AND LOOK BACK AT THOSE EARLY DAYS WITH GREAT FONDNESS. EVEN THE TOUGH SPOTS.
DO I HAVE REGRETS? SURE. WHO DOESN'T?
I SAW DANNY PERFORM WITH ALVIN AILEY. HE WAS AMAZING.
I WAS TOO SHY TO TRY AND SAY HI.
WHAT IS IT?
I THOUGHT I SAW SOME-ONE...
AN OLD FRIEND.

RUDIE MOVED UP TO THE CITY LAST YEAR, AND WE FORMED A SIDE REGGAE BAND FOR FUN.
WE GET HECKLED AND BOOED BY DIE-HARD ***PROPER LADY*** FANS, AND THEY ASK US IF WE'RE STILL FEMINISTS...
YOU JUST HAVE TO LAUGH SOMETIMES.
I'M NOT A SLOGAN. I'M NOT A T-SHIRT.
FREE
BREAKFAST LUNCH DINNER
I DON'T NEED A LABEL. EVEN ONE OF MY OWN DESIGN.

I MANAGE THIS COFFEE HOUSE IN THE EAST VILLAGE.
SPEAK UP!
IT PAYS THE RENT AND GIVES ME TIME TO MAKE MUSIC AND BE POLITICAL.
NO, I'M NOT RICH.
NO, I'M NOT FAMOUS.
I'M NOT A LOT OF THINGS.

FRIDAY, MAY 17
FEATURING
and introducing
The Proper Ladies
ALL AGES
BIKINI KILL!!
AT THE
BUT I'M HAPPY.

Emmett Helen

In between stints as a RICK AND MORTY cover artist, Emmett Helen has created short works for SWEATY PALMS, the LIFE FINDS A WAY anthology, DRAW OUT THE VOTE, and THE BEAUTIFUL BOOK OF EXQUISITE CORPSES. They spend hours in the kitchen and miss the beach just terribly. MY RIOT is their debut graphic novel.

Rick Spears

Rick Spears has written numerous graphic novels and comics including, TEENAGERS FROM MARS, BLACK METAL, and THE AUTEUR. He's also written for film, television, and directed a handful of award-winning short films. He lives in Richmond, Virginia, with his wife, son, and schnauzer.